British Museum Manuscript

**Vita Haroldi**

The Romance of the Life of Harold, King of England

British Museum Manuscript

**Vita Haroldi**
*The Romance of the Life of Harold, King of England*

ISBN/EAN: 9783337030858

Printed in Europe, USA, Canada, Australia, Japan

Cover: Foto ©ninafisch / pixelio.de

More available books at **www.hansebooks.com**

# THE ROMANCE OF THE LIFE

OF

# HAROLD, KING OF ENGLAND.

*From the Unique Manuscript in the British Museum.*

EDITED,

*WITH NOTES AND A TRANSLATION,*

BY

## WALTER DE GRAY BIRCH, F.S.A.,

*Senior Assistant in the Department of Manuscripts in the British Museum;
Honorary Secretary of the British Archæological Association;
Member of the Committee of the Palæographical Society, etc.*

LONDON: ELLIOT STOCK,
62, PATERNOSTER ROW, E.C.
1885.

# INTRODUCTION,

THE romantic life of King HAROLD—the laſt monarch before England fell under a ſeries of dominations of foreign dynaſties, which has laſted nearly nine hundred years—has, for a conſiderable time, formed an intereſting theme with hiſtorians and men of literature. It is printed in the following pages from a careful collation with the unique manuſcript in the Harley Library of the Britiſh Muſeum, No. 3776, with a tranſlation for the firſt time.

For the convenience of reference, I ſhall divide the ſubject of this introduction into the following ſections: (1) Deſcription of the Manuſcript; (2) Hiſtory of the Manuſcript; (3) Notices of the Hiſtorical Points, and of the Tranſlation.

## I. DESCRIPTION OF THE MANUSCRIPT.

The manuſcript is of quarto ſize, meaſuring $10\frac{3}{8}$ inches by 8 inches, of ſomewhat thick and rough vellum. The writing, in pale-coloured ink, is contained in thirty-one lines to a page, in a Gothic or black-letter book hand, occafionally difficult to interpret, becaufe of the fimilar way of forming the *m, ni, ui, in,* etc. It is evidently written, or rather copied from the author's own writing, by a fcribe ignorant of Latin—perhaps a novice of the great Abbey of Waltham—for feveral words are found divided erroneoufly, and others occur where they are improperly joined together. The ink, originally black, is now of a faded brown colour. The ornamental initial letters at the beginning of paragraphs are of red or blue colour; and the rubrics, or contents of chapters, are in red. The writing is of the latter end of the thirteenth century, or, at lateft, of the beginning of the fourteenth century.

The volume, of which the "Vita Haroldi" forms the firft article, contains feveral other treatifes, written by the fame fcribe, which have been difturbed at fome time from their original order of production, and other works have been introduced, although they have no connection with Waltham. The Waltham treatifes are numbered by the fcribe in numerical order, fo that we can readily reconftruct the arrangement of the volume when it repofed upon the quiet fhelves of the fcriptorium of that great monaftery. The fubjoined table fhows the contents of the work:

*Introduction.* vii

| Numeration of the Waltham Library. | Numeration of the Harley Library. | | Folio |
|---|---|---|---|
| 1. | (1) | Vita Haroldi ... | 1–24 |
| 2. | (2) | Ista quæ secuntur ... deficiunt in Libro de Inventione Crucis nostre de Waltham, etc. ... | 25–30 |
| 5. | | List of reliques brought by Harold to Waltham Abbey, etc. (*Lat.*)... | 31–35*b* |
| 6. | | Miracles performed by the wood of the Holy Cross at the altar of St. John the Evangelist, etc. (*Lat.*) ... | 35*b*–38 |
| 7. | | Verses on Waltham Abbey; Names of the Abbots, etc.; Visions, etc. (*Lat. and French*) ... | 38–42 |
| 8. | | A tract on the Invention of the Holy Cross of Waltham ... | 43–62 |
| | *(3) | A short chronicle of England from | |

\* Numbers 3 to 7 have been added to the volume; they are not of the same size, and are of later date. There is no evidence connecting them with Waltham.

| Numeration of the Waltham Library. | Numeration of the Harley Library. | | Folio |
|---|---|---|---|
| | | 1066 to 1128 (*Lat.*) ... ... | 63-66 |
| | *(4) | Life of St. Brandan (*Lat.*) ... ... | 67-75*b* |
| | *(5) | Henry of Saltrey's "Purgatory of St. Patrick" (*Lat.*) ... | 75*b*-82 |
| | *(6) | Life of Tungal, Bifhop of Cafhel (*Lat.*) ... ... | 82-89*b* |
| | *(7) | Three Vifions of Hell, etc. (*Lat.*) ... | 89*b*-92 |
| .2. | (8) | Meditation of St. Bonaventura, Minifter - General of the Minorite Friars (*Lat.*) ... | 94-114 |
| .3. | | Philofophical treatifes on fobriety; old age, etc. (*Lat.*) | 114*b*-116*b* |
| | (9) | Verfes on "Quid eft Femina." This, although made a feparate article, in the Harley catalogue, is part of the old numeration 3. It ends abruptly at the bottom of the page | 116*b*-117 |

*Introduction.* ix

| Numeration of the Waltham Library. | Numeration of the Harley Library. | | Folio |
|---|---|---|---|
| | *(10) | "Martilogium sanctorum in Anglia." A later tract on the burial-places of English saints (*Lat.*) ... ... | 118-128 |
| | *(11) | A calendar of the Saints' days and festivals, between two fly-leaves, from a service book (*Lat.*) ... ... | 129-135 |

## II. History of the Manuscript.

Of the authorship of this early tale (whether true or legendary we may never know) nothing is known for certain. Internal evidences point to the probability that it was composed about a hundred and fifty years after the battle of Hastings. Sir Thomas Duffus Hardy (whose account of the Codex is given in his "Descriptive Catalogue of Manuscripts relating to the Early History of Great Britain," vol. i., pp. 668-671) states that in his opinion "there is probably some truth in this curious narrative, but its errors are great and numerous. It is, however, known from good evidence that there was a report in circulation at an early period that Harold had escaped from the

* These two articles have never belonged to the Waltham MS.

slaughter at Hastings;" and he refers to Brompton,[1] Knyghton,[2] Ælred of Rievaulx,[3] and Giraldus Cambrensis,[4] those who are curious to know more on this subject. It is unnecessary to pursue this aspect of the subject on this occasion, for the object in view is not to theorize upon a matter which, after all that can be said on both sides, must yet remain unsolved. The endeavour of the present work is to present to the reader, in a convenient form, a text carefully collated from the only manuscript known to exist at the present time, with a translation appended to it (as literal as the remarkable style and phraseology, obscure, and in many places absolutely unintelligible, as it is, will allow it to be, but yet not slavishly close so as to be uninteresting to the general reader), for the use of those who cannot read it in the original Latin in which it is composed.

From what religious house the Manuscript passed ultimately into the hands of the great collector of the Harley Library is not, indeed, difficult to conjecture.

Here, again, Sir Thomas D. Hardy advances a fact which is highly probable. That learned palæographer considers that the composition was written apparently with the object of proving that Harold was not buried at Waltham, the traditional place of his sepulture, which, indeed, made that great House of Secular Canons rich and famous in the annals of British Monasticism. Now, as there

---

[1] *Chronicle*, col. 961.  [2] Col. 2342.
[3] P. 394.  [4] P. 874.

is little doubt that the work itfelf was compofed, and certainly as far as the prefent manufcript is concerned, no doubt at all that it was tranfcribed, in the Abbey of Waltham, it is difficult to conceive any means for accounting for the apparent anomaly of an eftablifhment which owed its profperity, in a vital degree, to the pious fentiments which cluftered around the fanctified fepulchre of the unfortunate King, caufing a tranfcript, or perhaps more than one, to be made of a treatife founded upon a fact, and profeffing to prove a fact, which, if generally accepted, would have utterly deftroyed the cultus of the departed monarch on which the flourifhing condition of the Abbey both morally and financially depended.

Hardy, confcious of this difficulty, fuggefts that the authorfhip of this work—here defignated by him as "little elfe than an hiftorical romance"—muft be attributed to "one of the fecular canons who had been expelled from that eftablifhment, and with the intention of robbing it of the honour of holding the remains of its founder." But when we come to examine the theory thus advanced, it falls to the ground, for even if we admit the fuggeftion of authorfhip at the date to which he fays internal evidence points—viz., one hundred and fifty years after the battle of Haftings, A.D. 1066 + 150 = A.D. 1216, as tolerably accurate,[1]—can we poffibly admit that, after giving the manufcript a

[1] The probability of this date is borne out in feveral paffages to which footnotes are given in the places where they occur.

place in the *scriptorium* or library of the Abbey for nearly two hundred years, during which time every inmate would have conftant accefs to a work which could not fail to aroufe his intereft and excite his critical comments, if not to fhake his faith in the orthodox ftory of his founder's fortunes, the authorities of that inftitution would permit a tranfcript fuch as this undoubtedly is, an unpolifhed, almoft, we may fay, an uncorrected copy to be made about the beginning of the fourteenth century?

### III. Notice of the Historical Points; and of the Translation.

In this unique MS., which has been carefully collated for the prefs, there are few points to which the attention of the reader may conveniently be directed here. The fimple *e* is ufed in all cafes for the *æ* or *œ* of ftandard Latin orthography; *h* is occafionally added to fuch words as *abundo*, where the afpirate is manifeftly an error, its addition, no doubt, marking the peculiar pronunciation of Latin by our infular fcholars at the time when this manufcript was prepared. Another interefting deviation from the claffical form, but one which is very reprefentative of the early mediæval period, is the ufe of the forms *reicio*, *eicio*, etc., for *rejicio*, *ejicio*, etc., where the *j* is eliminated from its proper place between two vowels. Set is ufed generally for *Sed*.

The punctuation is peculiar: no rules appear

to have guided the compofer, who puts a point (.), the equivalent of our comma (,), in many places where we fhould certainly not ufe any ftop; the colon (:) is alfo frequently placed dividing words from each other in paffages where the modern ideas of punctuation would not allow fuch a practice. The comma and the femicolon are unknown; but the inverted femicolon (؛) is occafionally ufed, much more fparingly than the point and the colon, in places where we fhould expect to fee the femicolon or comma.

The text in the following pages reprefents the actual reading of the MS. I have preferred to retain even manifeft errors in this text rather than attempt to explain them by any alteration. Moft of thefe errors, after all, eafily explain themfelves. The footnotes are marked H., to fhow that the readings are thofe of this Harley Manufcript. The collations are:

(i.) With the text, printed by M. Francifque Michel in his *Chroniques Anglo-Normandes, recueil d'Extraits et d'Ecrits relatifs à l'Hiftoire de Normandie et d'Angleterre*, 8vo., Rouen, 1835, Tome ii., pp. 143-222.

The text of chapters viii. and xii. are omitted by M. Michel, whofe text is otherwife fairly accurate and faithful. Where the readings of this edition are quoted in my footnotes, they are diftinguifhed by the letter M.

(ii.) With a very poorly edited copy of the above text in the *Chroniques*, by Rev. Dr. Giles, of C. C. C. Oxford, in his *Vita Quorundam*

*Anglo-Saxonum*, " Original Lives of Anglo-Saxons and others who lived before the Conqueſt." This work, which was printed and publiſhed for the Caxton Society by J. Ruſſell Smith, 1854, is now out of print. The remarkable peculiarities which the editor evinced in abſurdly endeavouring to reduce the orthography of the manuscript to what he fancied was a claſſical ſtandard, his careleſſneſs in failing to conſult the text of the MS. where the accuracy of the text of the *Chroniques* was doubtful, and the inaccuracies [1] with which his work abounds —culminating in his ludicrous footnote concerning his inability to point to the identification of a well-known locality in Shropſhire—combine to render the text he gives in the *Vita* abſolutely uſeless for purpoſes of critical examination or for quotation. I have collated a large number of theſe numerous departures from the true reading of the MS. in footnotes diſtinguiſhed by the letter G.

The tranſlation of this manuscript into Engliſh is here, as has been ſaid before, for the firſt time attempted. And here I have to thank my colleague, Mr. I. H. Jeayes, for considerable aſſiſtance in the work. The peculiar ſtyle and diction, involved and obſcure as it is almoſt throughout the work (except in a few narrative paſſages where the author condeſcends to write in a lucid and ſuccinct manner), occaſionally takes ſuch

---

[1] The firſt word of his title, *Vita* for *Vitæ*, ſhows the ſame careleſſneſs which runs through the whole of the work.

wandering flights of fancy that, even if we accept the readings of the scribe who made this Harley MS. as always correct—a fact which is by no means sure, for no second copy is extant with which to compare them—it is almost impossible to divine what the author wished to intimate to his hearers and readers, veiled and hidden in sentences of great length, crowded with "sesquipedalian words," and overflowing with that peculiar characteristic of antithesis which the Anglo-Saxon and early English literary man so strongly affected.

W. DE GRAY BIRCH.

*December*, 1884.

# VITA HAROLDI REGIS.

*Incipit Prologus in vita viri venerabilis Haroldi quondam Anglorum regis.*

SICUT federis tabernaculi fub Moyfe . ut templi fub Salomone Dominici . divine commendant littere conftructores : ita et eos profecuntur laudibus . qui devocione prona offerre aut preparare conftruccioni neceffaria: fideliter ftuduerunt. Apud Neemiam[1] qui deriferunt edificantes inprecacione terribili percelluntur. Reedificatores Ierufalem . titulis ab Hefdra perpetuis afcripti: nominis et operis fui perhennem pofteris memoriam confecrarunt. Hujufmodi confideracio ad ferendum qualecunque fuffragium operi fanéto in quo defudatis patres reverendi tenuem licet cenfu et viribus imbecillem parvitatem meam : vehementer vere fateor incitavit. Accedit ftimulo huic calcarium infuper vice jam ultro currenti . hinc fraterna cum amica fuafione poftulacio . inde cum paterna juffione follicita commonicio. Sencio quidem laboris plenum . fet mercede fpero refertum . et quod vefter

MS. Harl. 3776, f. 1.

[1] Nehem. vi.

nutus injungit . et quod nofter animus geftit. Expetendus autem fummoque nifu cenfetur amplectendus modici fudor temporis . quo non exigui et labentis evi celebritas: immo laudis et glorie eo manfure quo eterne decus et fplendor optinetur. Ceterum quovis pro labore aut opere . laudis tranfitorie expetiffe mercedem : operam perdidiffe eft et impenfam. Non folum autem fed nec nullatenus expetite ultro tamen ingefte adquieviffe favoris illecebre interni teftis et eterni judicis feipfum retribucione et laude privaffe eft. Extat enim de ejufmodi : ejufdem diffinicio hunc habens modum: Amen[1] dico vobis : receperunt mercedem fuam.

Jubet igitur ac petit auctoritas paterna . et fraterna caritas veftra quatinus opus egregium quod ceptum excellenter decenterque provectum . laudabilem[2] inftanter urgetis ad terminum . fumptibus invigilem hinc inde affumptis promovere . ne forte piis defint o[peri]bus copie neceffarie ad hoc perficiendum. Ex variis nempe patrum fcriptis volumen infigne in modulum unius libri compactum . ad laudem et de laude gloriofe ac deifice crucis operiofius elaboratum geftis memorabilibus[3] fundatoris veftri[4] . cujus memoria in benedictione eft . cupitis infigniri . talique ut ita dicatur celeumate laborem votivum confummari. Laudabile procul dubio quia devotum . quia providum hac in parte : fanctitatis veftre defiderium. Eft quidem devocionis nec indebite quod tanti viri magnalia nafciture preoptatis pofteritati litterarum

[1] Matt. vi. 2, 5.  [2] H. ; laudabile, G.M.
[3] H.M. ; memorabilibus, G.  [4] H.M. ; noftri, G.

indiciis fideliter affignare. Eo quippe juris tenore peculiarem patronum et perpetuum nutritorem veftrum debitis tenemini virtutum fuarum preconiis illuftrare . quo crimini poterat ingratitudinis non oblique afcribi : fi promeritos[1] laudum ipfius titulos . editui fui et alumpni defidiofo filencio pofteris furarentur. Providencie nichilominus competentis eft quod laudibus fancte crucis ipfius cultoris devotiffimi laudes decernitis fubrogandas. Crucis fancte ex toto nimirum accedit glorie quicquid in fervi fui meritis et virtutibus: enituit commendabile.

Inter hec quam mee pariter incumbat modicitati animo magno et volenti quicquid vires fuggefferint immo quicquid gratia celeftis indulferit ad impendia tam boni operis haut[2] fegniter corrogare quis nefciat ? Veftrum fiquidem immo Haroldi veftri quinimmo fancte utrorumque crucis jamdiu panem comedens ociofus . quo veftros erga me fereniores vultus afpicio: eo in me feveriorem illorum fenfuram[3] pertimefcere jure debeo . fi tantis quod abfit beneficiis non dixerim ingratum fet[4] inofficiofum . tam gratis quam graciofe exhibitum : contingat inveniri. Geram igitur morem veftris pro poffe defideriis geram quam potero vicem beneficiis: ea tamen racione quatinus et vos veftra michi pacta fervetis. Tenorem fcilicet fcribendorum diligentius examinetis . examinata tantummodo approbetis : aut emendetis. Sermonis quoque

---

[1] Pro meritos, MS., with mark by a late hand to join the words.  [2] H.M.; haud, G.
[3] Sic MS.; cenfuram, G.  [4] Sed, G.

## Vita Haroldi Regis.

reicientes[1] minus elimati rufticitatem . fententiam fi videbitur refervetis[2] eleganciori ut dignum eft ftilo explicandam. Nec enim defunt largiente Domino cetui fanctitatis veftre Befeleelis[3]. Ooliab[4]. feu Hyram[5] peritiffimi fucceffores . qui oblatam in donaria Domini a fupplici vulgo rudem materiam . locis et ufibus congruentibus noverint adaptare. Noverint quoque arte magiftra prout res exigit fingula queque fubtilius expolire . refecare fuperflua informia componere: deformia exornare. Mee vero tantifper intererit impericie . aptiorem fabrice materiam a montibus excifam . et ratibus impofitam . ad planiora deducere. Quod egiffe putabor fi a prifcorum libris . fi a fedulis[6] modernorum . fi a quorumdam fidelium relacionibus veris . paffim collecta: hujus libelli apicibus

---

[1] Rejicientes, G.      [2] Referventes, G.
[3] Befeleel I. anno mundi 2544 . ante Jefum Chriftum 1510 . filius Uri et Marie fororis Moyfis . de tribu Juda. Hunc ipfum elegit Dominus cum Ooliab . de tribu Dan . quos implevit fpiritu Dei . fapientia et intelligentia . et fcientia in omni opere ad excogitandum quidquid fabrefieri poterat ex auro et argento . et ere . marmore et gemmis . et diverfitate lignorum . ad edificandum tabernaculum foederis . arcam teftimonii . propitiatorium . et cuncta vafa tabernaculi. (F. P. Dutripon, 'Concordantiæ,' Paris, 1844, p. 157.) Befeleel's name occurs in Exod. xxxi. 2 ; xxxv. 30; xxxvi. 1 ; xxxvii. 1 ; xxxviii. 22 ; 1 Par. ii. 20 ; 2 Par. i. 5.
[4] Ooliab . filius Achifamech a tribu Dan. Artifex a Deo vocatus . fpirituque Sapientie et intelligentie impletus ad edificationem tabernaculi una cum Befeleel. (Dutripon, *ut fupra*, p. 983.) Ooliab occurs in Exod. xxxi. 6 ; xxxv. 34 ; xxxvi. 1 ; xxxviii. 23.
[5] Hiram . artifex erarius plenus fapientia, etc. (Dutripon, *ut fupra*, p. 607.) Hiram occurs by name in 3 Reg. vii. 13 ; xl. 45 ; 2 Par. ii. 13 ; iv. 11, 16.
[6] H.M.; fchedulis, G.

que injungitis tradidero: fimplicium noticie profutura. Oracionum autem veftrarum aura lenis et placida fragilem eloquii noftri cimbam crucis vexillo pro velo . et jufti fui precibus pro ampluftribus[1] inftructam: in portum fecundi litoris perducat. Amen.

[1] Ampliis tribus, M.; apluftribus, G.

## EXPLICIT PROLOGUS.

## INCIPIUNT CAPITULA.

PRIMUM. Quod fpeculum ferenitatis et clemencie eluceat in geftis regis Haroldi. Quod frater regine fuit . quam fanctus duxit Edwardus. Qualiter pater ejus Godwinus dolum eludens Cnutonis regis . fororem ipfius accepit in uxorem . et quod de viciis nutritorum fuorum Haroldus infigniter triumphaverit.

II. Quod Wallia per Haroldum pene deleta fit: et qualiter ipfe per virtutem Sancte Crucis de Waltham de paralifi[1] convaluerit.

III. Quomodo ecclefiam Sancte Crucis apud Waltham conftruxerit . ditaverit . ornaverit . atque ordinaverit Haroldus . et quod Henricus Anglorum rex amotis fecularibus ipfum locum canonicis infignivit regularibus.

IV. Quod divinitus difpofitum fuit ut homo ifte in regem erigeretur . et victis hoftibus ab eo: ab aliis ipfe victus a regno deiceretur . et de anachorita valde religiofo qui minifter ipfius jam folitarii fuerat.

V. Quod inter vulneratores feminecem inventum et Wintoniam perductum . mulier quedam

---

[1] H.M.; paralyfi, G.

Saracena biennio ibidem delitefcentem fanaverit Haroldum . et quod pro contrahendis contra Normannos auxiliis . Saxones Dacofque expetierit nilque profecerit.

VI. Quod in fe tandem idem reverfus intellexerit Deum fibi in via mundi adverfari . unde Chrifti fe conformans cruci ut hoftem antiquum melius triumpharet gaudet fe ab hominibus fuiffe fuperatum.

VII. Quod pro expeciendis[1] fanctorum fuffragiis longam inierit peregrinacionem: et quod antequam regnum habuiffet . fanctorum limina apoftolorum adierit.

VIII. Ammiracio[2] fcriptoris cum exclamacione brevi fuper benignitate Dei qua fit ut etiam peccata electorum: ipfis cooperentur in bonum.

NONUM. Quod de peccato Haroldi multa dicuntur a multis: et de quercu fecus Rothomagum fub qua juraverat . que corticem exuta manet ufque in prefens.

X. Satiffaccio quorundam pro Haroldo . qua eum de perjurio excufantes . Domino favente et fancto connivente Edwardo ipfum regnaffe affirmant . et de vifione Abbatis Elfini . qua victorem Norwagicorum ipfum fore prenunciavit fanctus Edwardus.

UNDECIMUM. De cruce fancta admirabilis quorum[3] relacio que regi Haroldo feftinanti ad prelium caput perhibetur inclinaffe et alia quedam fatis de ipfa cruce ftupenda miracula certiffime approbata.

XII. Diverforum diverfa interpretacio fuper predictis fignis crucis fe inclinantis et quercus arefacte . et quod Haroldus fe ipfum bene judicando

---

[1] H.M.; expetendis, G.   [2] H.M.; Admiratio, G.
[3] H.M.; quorundam, G.

judicium prevenerit divinum et non formidet humanum.

XIII. Quod multis in peregre[1] annis exactis[2] ad Angliam ob exercitandam pacienciam et benignitatem Haroldus rediens Chriftianum fe vocitari fecerit . decenniumque in rupe quadam expleverit folitarie vivens . et in hujus temporis antichriftos compendiofa inveccio.

XIIII. Quod in confinio Wallencium[3] poftmodum Haroldus pluribus in locis tempore multo degens . pacienter eorum frequencius tulerit affultus . faciem velans panno . et nomen nomine alio . ne aliquatenus cognofceretur quod tandem ad ejus veneracionem converfa eft immanitas perfecutorum.[4]

XV. Quod vir Domini Haroldus fugit obfequentes quos adierat et diu fuftinuerat perfequentes . et quod voce de celo lapfa defignatus fit ei locus paufacionis fue . et quod femiplenis verborum indiciis . fcifcitantibus innuerit fe fuiffe Haroldum et quod fcripto fucceffioris fui plenius oftendetur inferius hujus rei certitudo.

XVI. Monetur lector ne fpernat leccionem quam fentit a non nullorum[5] opinionibus difcrepare . et de triplici occafione contraria exiftimancium fuper materia prefenti . et de Willelmi Meldunelfis[6] circa Haroldi fata errore triformi.

XVII. Quid acciderit Waltammenfibus[7] circa

[1] Inperegre, M.G.
[2] H.M. ; extractis, G.   [3] H.M. ; Wallenfium, G.
[4] H.M. ; perfequutorum, G.
[5] H. ; nonnullorum, M.G.
[6] H.M. ; Meldunenfis, rightly, G.
[7] H.M. ; Walthammenfibus, G. The fcribe of the Harley MS. has written this word thus, "Waltā menfibus," clearly proving that he did not underftand what he was writing.

patroni fui sepulturam pie follicitis sed mulieris cujusdam errore delusis.

XVIII. Quid frater Haroldi Gurta nomine f. 3. Abbati Waltero vel aliis responderit super fratris sui requisitus cineribus vel sepultura.

XIX. Quod viri Dei successor de gestis Haroldi beatissimi vera scribens . causas gestorum minus congrue . bis assignaverit . et prime assignacionis discussio . et competens prolatis sentenciarum diviciarum[1] . testimoniis ejusdem improbacio.

XX. Secunde assignacionis infirmacio et scriptoris ad lectorem deprecacio et de difficultate materiam resarciendi a priscis scriptoribus varie laceratam.

[1] Diversarum, M.G.

## EXPLICIUNT CAPITULA.

*Quod speculum serenitatis et clemencie Dei eluceat in gestis regis Haro[l]di.*[1] *Quod frater regine fuit quam sanctus duxit Edwardus. Qualiter pater ejus Godwinus dolum eludens Cnutonis regis sororem ipsius accepit in uxorem . et quod de viciis nutritorum suorum Haroldus insigniter triumphaverit.*

## INCIPIT VITA SERVI DEI HARO[L]DI[1]. QUONDAM REGIS . ANGLORUM.

### Capitulum I.

LLUSTRISSIMI vere quia regis legitimi Haroldi jam rite ac legitime coronati gesta recensere . nichil[2] aliud est quam divine serenitatis simul et clemencie quasi speculum quoddam lucidissimum piis mentibus exhibere. Quod ut clareat manifestius: ipsius immundana[3] seu in Christi milicia primordium progressum et terminum dilucide curabimus summatimque legentibus intimare. Vere

[1] G.; Harodi, H. Haro[l]di, M.
[2] H.M.; Nihil, G.; and so in all cases throughout the text.
[3] In mundana, M.G.

autem regem illuftriffimum legittimeque[1] hunc dixerimus coronatum . qui fe ipfum bene regendo illique devotiffime cui fervire regnare eft obfequendo: coronam adeptus eft primum jufticie et poftmodum glorie fempiterne. Hunc Godwinus[2] comes potentiffimus . ex forore Cnutonis Anglorum pariter et Dacorum regis habuit filium fratrem vero regine venerabilis quam rex et confeffor fanctiffimus duxerat Edwardus. Cujus felici matrimonio quamquam citra opus juncta fuerit maritale utrifque nimirum permanentibus in perpetue virginitatis flore: promocionis tamen multimode caufa fuit paterne familie. Conftat vero

---

[1] H.M. ; legitimeque, G.

[2] It will be ufeful to introduce here a table fhowing the pedigree of Harold, Edward the Confeffor, and William the Conqueror, and their relationfhip with each other.

Richard I., 'Sans-Peur,' Duke of Normandy, d. 996.

| Richard II., 'Le Bon,' D. of Normandy, d. 1027. | (2.) in 1017, =Emma, Canute, K. of England and Denmark. | =(1.) in 1012, Ethelred II., K. of England, d. 1016. | d. 1054. | Godwin, Earl of Kent, d. 1053. |
|---|---|---|---|---|

| Richard III., D. of Normandy, d. 1028, s.p. | Robert I., 'Le Diable,' D. of Normandy, d. 1035. | Alfred, d. 1036. | EDWARD, 'The Confeffor,' K. of England, d. 1066. | =Edith, in 1044. | HAROLD II., E. of Kent, K. of England 1066, d. 1066. | =Aldgyth. |
|---|---|---|---|---|---|---|

| WILLIAM, 'The Conqueror,' born 1027, D. of Normandy 1035, K. of England 1066, d. 1087. | Gurth. | Godwin. | Edmund. | Magnus. | Ulf. | Harold. | Gytha. | =Wladimir, fon of Jaroflav, Grand-Duke of Ruffia, d. 1051. |
|---|---|---|---|---|---|---|---|---|

ipsius genitorem vel ceterorum quosdam de illius genere . tum¹ prodicionis tum¹ et aliorum nota facinorum infamatos² graviter fuisse.

Hiis³ vero malis . necessitate cavendi imminentis exicii : Godwinus se primo immiscuit deinde ulterius evagatur. Tuende siquidem salutis obtentu dolum temptare⁴ compulsus . dum semel cedit ad votum: fraudibus in posterum minuende felicitatis intuitu licencius nitebatur. Dum enim prefatus rex Dacie diadema Anglie usurpasset : cerneretque Godwinum incredibili astucia nec minori audacia preditum sensim ad sublimia conscendere timere cepit homo advena . indigene adolescentis viribus simul armatam et astu animositatem. Cujus licet sibi pernecessariam in multis expertam habuisset industriam: quiddam tamen de spiritu Saulis mente concipiens ereptorem suum propugnatoremque strenuissimum dolo perdere cogitavit . quem palam opprimere nisi per invidiosam maliciam facile non fuit. Excogitato igitur consilio Godwinum quasi pro arduis regni utriusque negociis mittit in Daciam . tale quid secum mente pertractans . Non sit super eum manus mea ; sed sit super eum manus Dacorum . cum⁵ igitur jam medium equor navi opulentissimo instructa apparatu secaret ; cepit suspicio juvenis animum vehemencius titillare . ferebat namque signatas regis anulo litteras . singulis scilicet illius terre optimatibus singulas . quarum

---

[1] H.G. ; tantum . . . tantum, M.
[2] M.G.; the letters *ama* in this word written in modern ink, H.
[3] H.M. ; His, G.    [4] H.M.; tentare, G.
[5] H.M. ; Quum, G ; and so throughout the text when used as a conjunction.

omnium prorsus nesciebat sentencias. Unius igitur sigillorum cautus effractor ex brevi incluso se in brevi agnoscit capitali dandum supplicio; si portitoris cum ventum fuerit ad portum plenius fungatur officio. Tenor enim scripture hic erat. ut quicumque illius seriem primitus advertisset. bajulum ejus Godwinum nomine capite incontinenti[1] mutilaret.

Expalluit novus Urias comperto quod sibi a rege parabatur. exicio paratque ut paucis utamur dolum extimplo[2] eludere dolo. fecit sic: extractasque a ceris suis singulas confregit cartulas[3]. callidaque clerici cujusdam manu reponit recentes. quarum summa fuit ut Godwinum summo universorum tripudio exceptum. regie sororis nupciis darent. nec aliter ei quam sibi si adesset in hiis[4] que regia exigebant negocia incunctanter cuncti parerent. Sic regis bono regia mutatur sentencia. sic miles milicie mutat stipendia. sic indebita cedit pena et debita bene merito accedit gloria. Sic denique in fratrem recipit quem utilem repperit rex militem. quem eciam paulo post fecit consulem habuitque pervigilem in reliquum provisorem.

Quo tamen eventu Godwinus in Dacorum plus quam satis favorem effusus. gentis sue quampluribus fiebat infestus.[5] Non nullos quoque de semine regio quorum unus frater Sancti Edwardi fuit dolo perdidit sicque non modo in concives. immo et in dominos naturales non pauca deliquit. Verum

Nota de Edwardo et Godwino Pascali tempore.

[1] H.M.G.; for incontinenter.  [2] H.M.; extemplo, G.
[3] H.M.; chartulas, G.  [4] H.; iis, M.G.
[5] In festus, H.

de hiis[1] alias qui voluerit plura inquirat. Quo[2] enim ad fusceptam attinet materiam . satis est iccirco nos vel compendiose ista prelibasse ne inconsulte videremur illa preterisse : que minus intelligentes ad servi Dei Haroldi contumeliam novimus intorsisse . cum sanum sapientes hec quam maxime ad ipsius gloriam videant pertinere. Qui enim gratia comitante divina vicium vicit quod ut isti volunt natura inflixit quod convictus instituit : eo utique favorabilius triumphavit . quo et hoc ipsum quod natus . quod educatus est : superando mutavit. Nam etsi vicio ipse quoque ut asseritur evo adhuc rudis cessisse visus est . a natura simul et nutritura . violenciam passus estimandus est. Patet igitur quia operante eo qui de eadem massa vas aliud facit in honorem . aliud in contumeliam . id quoque in virtutis Haroldo versum est meritum et laudis preconium quod ei ad vituperium ab indoctis fuerat objectum. Sic rutilos producit . sic niveos[3] quasi nutrit rosarum liliorumque : spina flores . quorum prerogative non adimit immo adicit[4] qualitas abjectior ex consorcio cumulum venustatis.

[1] H.M. ; his, G.  
[2] H.M. ; Quod, G.  
[3] H. ; niveas, M.G.  
[4] H.M. ; adjicit, G.

*Quod Wallia per Haroldum pene deleta sit; et qualiter ipse per virtutem Sancte Crucis de Waltham de paralisi[1] convaluerit . . . ij*

IRIBUS autem corporis quantum prestiterit quam acer et strenuus animis armisque innotuerit: subacta immo ad internicionem[2] per Haroldum pene deleta: Wallia est experta. In hiis[3] quidem triumphis . vivente adhuc sancto rege Edwardo: insignis enituit . Hiis regi et regno pacem et quietem quam fortiter tam et utiliter adquisivit. Interea dum inter coevos probitate et potencia major . summis eciam in regno proceribus prelacior esse videretur: manus omnipotentis que percutit et medetur carnem istius gravi percussione tetigit . ut sic presentibus necnon[4] et futuris anime ipsius vulneribus medelam procuraret. Paralisin[5] vocant medici genus morbi quo corpus hominis attactum debita dediscit officia . obsequia homini derogat consueta. Reddit enim subito partem quam invaserit . aut corporis totum: stupidum torpens

Nota de Ailardo Medico. f. 4 b.

---

[1] H.M.; paralysi, G.   [2] H.M.; internecionem, G.
[3] H.M.; his, G.; and so always throughout this text.
[4] H.; nec non, M.G.   [5] H.M.; Paralysin, G.

c

et quafi emortuum. Haroldus hac repente tactus
ac proftractus[1] moleftia ; cum ceteris effet merori
tum[2] prefertim regi: fit precipui caufa doloris.
Hunc enim velut quodam prefagio futurorum pre
ceteris carum habuit et dilectum ; cum ftirpis
illius quofdam fufpectos habuiffe dicatur aliquatenus et invifos. Quod fibi penes regem fanctiffi-
mum dileccionis et gracie privilegium non affini-
tatis quamlibet grata propinquitas non probitatis
non induftrie fingularis quibus erat preditus emi-
nentia ; immo fola celeftis infpiracio conciliaffe
eftimatur. Probabile enim fatis eft ad gloriam in
hac parte Haroldi quia vir Deo plenus. divinique in
multis confilii non ignarus eo indulgencius[3] ipfum
amaverit quo perpetuum in celis pocius coheredem
quam in terris fibi futurum previdebat momen-
taneum fucceflorem. Directi igitur regis a latere
medici, necnon et alii atque alii prece precioque
hinc inde allecti. egrotum ambiunt, quod ars feu
conjectura fuggerit exierunt[4]. fed Omnipotentis
manum vires hominum ammovere[5] non poffunt.
Pervenit fama triftior ad aures Alemannorum im-
peratoris. qui regi Anglorum affinitate proxi-
mus. dileccione et amicicia erat conjunctiffimus.
Huic medicus quidam nomine Ailardus fami-
liaris erat. quem et artis fue duplex exercicium
pericia et experiencia multa reddebat probatiffi-
mum. et quod pluris eft favor divinus in pro-
curanda fofpitate languencium : exhibuit graciofum.

[1] H.M.; proftratus, G.
[2] H.; tantun, M.; tantum, G.     [3] H.M.; diligentius, G.
[4] H.M.; excierunt, G.     [5] H.M.; amovere, G.

Hunc igitur imperator adhibendam[1] ſtrenuiſſimo juveni medelam: regi amantiſſimo celeriter deſtinavit. Qui ad egrum deductus egritudinis materiam ſagaciter rimatus curam adhibuit quam potuit. ſet[2] in ventum omnis cedit opera: ubi hominis artificio celeſtis opifex molitur adverſa.

Ea tempeſtate lapidea crucifixi regis noſtri ymago[3] non multis ante celitus revelata et reperta temporibus. et ad Waltham[4] nutu perlata divino: miris in loco virtutum choruſcabat[5] ſignis. Perpendens itaque phiſicus[6] nature auctorem naturalibus artis ſue viribus contraire. omnemque inferioris nature racionem. naturantis[7] nature prejudicio funditus hebetari; intellexit protinus hominem verbere conſtringi virtutis illius de cujus manu non eſt qui poſſit eruere. Qui mox ut virum decuit fidelem f. 5. et prudentem. cui manu nequivit: ore non diſtulit remedium procurare. Nil enim moris habens fallacium mencienciumque medicorum opem voluit a ſe ſeparari. quam ſenſit jam: per ſe non poſſe conferri. Nec ſuum tamen egrotum reliquid[8] deſperatum, ſet a ſpe vana in ſolidam hunc ſpem transferens. in eo ſperare qui ſalus eſt. ſperancium in ſe fideliter ſuadebat. A quo ut ocius optate ſalutis gaudia percipere mereretur: crucis ſalutifere ob-

---

[1] H.M.; ad adhibendam, G.
[2] H.M.; ſed, G.; and ſo always throughout.
[3] H.M.; imago, G.
[4] There are ſeveral intereſting tracts relating to the croſs at Waltham in the ſame Harley MS. from which this text is derived. For a mould, from which leaden badges of the Holy Croſs were caſt, ſee *Journal of the British Archæological Aſſociation*, vol. xxix. 421; cf. xxx. 52.
[5] H.M.; coruſcabat, G.      [6] H.M.; phyſicus, G.
[7] H.M.; naturantis, omitted, G.    [8] H.M.; reliquit, G.

sequiis hunc infistere . votumque illi vovere . prout sibi dictaret interna devocio: salubriter adhortatur. Languidus vero salutis confilium sano percepit animo . mittitque concito ad locum ubi crux virtuosa celebris radiabat: exennia[1] ingencia. Supplicat obnixius loci custodibus salutaris nimirum signi peculiarius cultui mancipatis . quatinus et criminum veniam et dolorum levamen utriusque videlicet hominis sospitatem sedulis sibi dignentur precibus optinere.[2] Nec defuit in longum clemencia salvatoris salutem a se fide non ficta postulanti. Mox etenim dolor cum languore decrevit a corpore amor vero cum devocione circa sancte crucis obsequium jam convalescenti mirabiliter crescebat in mente. In brevi siquidem plenissime redditus sospitati . quantum medicine qua[3] convaluerat extiterit devotus: magnificus[4] comprobavit operum documentis. Veniens enim ad sanctam crucem Waltamensem[5] salutaria curacionis sue vota persolvit donaria obtulit preciosa . ministris plurima largitus est . se ipsum gloriose crucis tutele commendans . hancque sublimius honorare disponens: letus tandem[6] a loco . non corde recedens sed corpore: domino Regi et sorori regine se incolumen[7] presentavit. Congratulatur fratri regina . rex militi congaudet: universa simul curia exultacione festiva letatur. Nec quia convaluit . set quia celitus receperat sanitatem: omnes quidem

---

[1] H.M.; exenia, G.
[2] H.M.; obtinere, G.   [3] H.; quam, M.; [per] quam, G.
[4] H.M.; magnificis, G.   [5] H.M.; Walthamienfem, G.
[6] H.; tamen, M.G.   [7] H.; incolumem, M.G.

in commune . plaudebant fet rex ut erat fanctiffimus impenfius gratulatur. Geminata fiquidem
letitia pre ceteris triumphabat . qui et Chrifti de-
lectabatur virtutibus tam pia exhibentis et devocionis[1] fideique profectibus pafcebatur in illis: quos
talium exhibicio in amore folidabat ejufdem piiffimi
Redemptoris.

[1] H.; dovocionis, M.; devotionis, G.

*Quomodo ecclesiam Sancte Crucis apud Waltham construxerit . ditaverit . ornaverit . atque ordinaverit Haroldus et . quod Henricus Anglorum rex amotis secularibus locum ipsius Canonicis insignivit regularibus.* . . . . *iij.*

AM vero hunc in quo vel per quem virtus experta . et ostensa virtutis prebuit tam multis incentivum nil aliud cogitare nil loqui perpenderes: nisi qualiter divinis posset beneficiis excellencius congruenciusque respondere qualiter honore condigno salutis adepte gaudia . sancte quivisset cruci compensare. Quo impensius autem ejus intendebat cultui et insistebat decori . eo sublimius gracia illum celestis virtutum et devocionis ditabat incrementis. Qua vir nobilis commercii specie magnopere delectatus . contendebat instancius de perceptis muneribus gracias exhibendo beneficia mereri pociora. Intuetur preterea quia et viro illi ad gracias non exiles teneretur . per quem superna pietas tot sibi exordia referasset commodorum: decernitque condigno hunc fidei sue et devocionis premio munerandum. Custodie siquidem oratorii

crucis adorande duo tantum clerici tam brevibus ftipendiis quam tectis contenti humilibus videbantur infervire. At vir magnificus locum et loci cultum omnimodis cupiens cum fuis cultoribus fublimare novam ibi bafilicam fabricare . miniftrorum augere numerum redditufque[1] eorum proponit ampliare. Utque celebriorem fama illuftriorem clericorum frequencia . celeftibus nobilitatum muneribus locum terrigenis exhiberet: fcolas[2] ibidem inftitui fub regimine magiftri Ailardi fue ut prelibatum eft falutis miniftri: difpoficione fatagebat prudenti. Nec paulo fegnius quod mente conceperat rerum pergebat effectibus parturire. Jaciuntur feftinato ecclefie amplioris fundamenta . furgunt parietes . columpne[3] fublimes . diftantes ab invicem parietes . arcuum aut teftudinum emicidiis mutuo federantur. Culmen impofitum aeris ab introgreffis plumbei objective laminis: variam fecludit intemperiem. Binarius clericorum numerus fcilicet infamis: in mifticum[4] fenatus apoftolici duodenarium convalefcet.[5] Pulcherrima nimirum racione ut totidem in ejus templo fancte crucis laudibus perhenniter[6] infervirent perfone quot illius gloriam mundo princi- f. 6. paliter ab inicio homines nunciaffent. Hiis vero predia et poffeffiones unde fibi ad omnem fufficienciam neceffaria provenirent liberali munificencia contulit regia quoque auctoritate confirmari optinuit.[7]

---

[1] H.M.; reditufque, G.  [2] H.M.; fcholas, G.
[3] H.M.; columnæ, G.  [4] H.M.; myfticum, G.
[5] M.; convalefcit, G.; -cet altered to -cit, H.
[6] H.M.; perenniter, G.  [7] H.M.; obtinuit, G.

Jam si temptemus[1] stilo[2] evolvere quot donariis[3] quam preciosis et multiplicibus vasis et ornamentis vario instructam decore illam edem Dominicam nobilitaverit . fidem scribendis forsan derogabit tantarum rerum multitudo. Verum ne funditus vel in hac parte magnificencie illius memoria deleatur ad quod tamen livor vehemencius aspirasse cognoscitur: opere precium est pro zeli fervore obniti . et cum species[4] ipse rerum sublate sunt quasdam velut umbras ipsarum considerare volentibus intimare. Indicium proinde rerum illarum que a primo Normannici generis Anglorum rege Willelmo in Haroldi ut traditur invidiam sancte sue crucis ecclesie violenter ablate . et in Neustriam translate sunt: presenti duximus pagine inferendum. Transtulit enim ut legitur idem rex de Waltham in Normanniam septem scrinia . ubi tria fuerunt aurea et quatuor argentea deaurata: cum gemmis preciosis plena reliquiarum . Quatuor textus: auro argento . gemmisque[5] ornatos . Quatuor turibula magna: aurea atque argentea . Sex candelabra: quorum duo aurea cetera argentea . Tres urceos magnos ex Greco opere: argenteos atque deauratos. Quatuor cruces auro atque argento et gemmis: fabricatas . Unam crucem ex quinquaginta marcis argenti fusilem . Quinque vestimenta sacerdotalia preciosissima: auro gemmisque ornata . Quinque casulas auro gemmisque ornatas: in una quarum

NOTA.
Summa . vj .
milibus et . vj .
centis et . lxvj .
libris. Scilicet
in cappis aureis
et argenteis . in
crucibus textis .
et casulam que
vocata est :—
Dominus dixit
ad me.

---

[1] H.M. ; tentemus, G.
[2] H.M. ; stylo, G. ; and so always in the cases of this word.
[3] See this MS. fol. 31, where a considerable list is given.
[4] H.M. ; speices, G.
[5] H.G. ; an erasure in H., gemmi$^s_z$.

erant duodecim marce auri . Duas capas: auro
gemmifque ornatas . Quinque calices: duos aureos
ceteros argenteos . Quatuor altaria cum reliquiis:
quorum unum aureum cetera argentea deaurata.
Unum cornu vinacium argenteum . centum folidis
computatum . Decem philacteria . unum quorum
de duabus marcis auri: et gemmis preciofis .
cetera: auro argentoque parata . Duas fambucas
fellas femineas: ex multo auro fabricatas . Duas
campanas: preciofas . Hec et alia permulta que f. 6 b.
longum effet referre . queque Normannorum
ambicio incomparabilia eftimaret . devote per
Haroldum fancte cruci oblata et per Willelmum
invidiofe nofcuntur ablata. Hujus tamen abla-
cionis invidiam perfunctoria quadam vifus eft idem
Willelmus compenfacione palliaffe ficut infcriptum
illa plenius refertur qua de invencione fancte fepius
memorate crucis edita . ordinem quoque quo ad
Waltham perlata eft ipfa crux: luculenter infinuat.
Ubi eciam que et quanta loco fancto five in prediis
et variis redditibus[1] five in rebus multiplicibus ad
minifterium vel ornatum ecclefie pertinentibus .
mirabili devocionis ardore contulerit vir pius:
plenius reperitur expreffum. Nam quia ftilus ad
ea properat explicanda que cultor crucis geffit ac
pertulit poftquam fe ipfum in holocauftum Domino
fuaviffimum optulit[2] tollens jam quotidie crucem
fuam et Chriftum fequens . pauca de hiis[3] perftri-
gendo referimus que de rebus fuis velut facrificium

[1] H.M.; reditibus, G.; and fo always in the cafes of this word.

[2] H.M.; obtulit, G.; and fo always in the various forms of this verb. [3] H.M.; iis, G.

justicie: Cruci confecrata donavit. Quorum tam multis in rebus mobilibus illi fublatis quecumque in terris . et villis[1] five ecclefiis aliifque redditibus loco affignavit hactenus fine diminucione magna non attamen fine nulla ut dicitur poffidere videtur. Statum vero ecclefie Walthamenfis per dive recordacionis regem Henricum fecundum in optimum noftris modo temporibus gradum videmus reformatum.[2] Canonici namque fub rigida . et difciplinabili regula ecclefiafticis excubiis per Haroldum mancipati ad fecularia fenfim tractu temporis plus equo devoluti facro canoni pretulerant vanitatem feculi. Nomen enim trahentes de utroque feculo videlicet et canone: perverfo ordine rem nominis dimidiavere. Secundum[3] namque fpiritantes et canonem fpernentes . hujus fcita et illius oblectamenta: lance librabant minus equa . unde pofthabitis divinis officiis fpaciabantur in triviis mundi: quibus verfandum erat in atriis domus Domini. Quibus demum pio regis jam dicti zelo inde amotis regularibus canonicis locus idem nobiliter infignitur. Qui Greco bene canoni regulam jungentes Latinam . fic gemine vocis et rei fimplicis virtutem vivendo teneunt[4] . quod Grecis jure et Latinis maxime veneracioni effe deberent. Hos Henricus officinis regularibus venuftiffime decoravit: fet Haroldus redditibus[5] neceffariis gratiffime

---

[1] H. ; et villis, omitted, M.G.

[2] This paffage clearly indicates that the prefent text was written after the death of King Henry II., 6 July, A.D. 1189.

[3] Sic MS. Sedm̄ for Sclm̄ ; with a marginal note *Seculum;* Seculum, M.G.

[4] M.G.; tenent, G.       [5] H.M. ; reditibus, G.

sublimavit. Hiis enim sustentatur grex Dominicus f. 7.
in sanctitate et justicia ibidem Domino devotissime
serviens; hiis cotidie[1] adventancium caterve innu-
merabiles: multimoda consequantur[2] humanitatis
bona. Hiis viatores[3] hiis famelicus: victum et
viaticum hiis languens: curam hiis algens; tegmen.
hiis tectum: hospes et advena. Hiis denique omnis
egens . necessitati sue subsidia recepit oportuna.[4]

[1] H.M.; quotidie, G.   [2] H.M.; consequuntur, G.
[3] H.; viator, M.G.   [4] H.M.; opportuna, G.

*Quod divinitus dispositum fuit ut homo iste in regem erigeretur et aliis victis hostibus ab eo . ab aliis ipse victus a regno deiceretur . et de Anachorita valde religioso qui minister ipsius jam solitarii fuerat.* . . . . . *iiij*

UIS novit hominum quomodo compingantur ossa hominis in ventre pregnantis? Quis vero scivit vel scire poterit . quid conducat homini in vita sua? Dominatur plerumque homo homini in malum suum. Deprimitur nonnunquam et subicitur ab homine homo homini: in bonum suum. Sic in servum servorum fratribus suis addicitur Chanaan . sic manus Joseph fraterno addicte zelo : in Chophmo servierunt. Sic et Haroldus noster ut ad propositum redeamus tanquam super ventum subito elevatur et repente eliditur valide. Regno pariter acclamante in regem erigitur . cesis qui irruperant barbaris victor ab acie cum triumpho revertitur. Recentem supervenisse hostem ut audit non metuit . sed insultat exterminatori suo veluti protinus exterminando occursitat. Manus conserit: et concidit congreditur et consciditur. Consciditur quidem et concidit . set

numquid ad perniciem vel ad infipienciam fibi? Num hoc fuftinebit manus illa regis crucifixi . qua obftetricante egreffus eft coluber tortuofus? ea quidem permittente tetigit offa ejus . et fingula fere membra hoftilis framea . carnem quoque ejus graviter vulneravit. Hac difpenfante hac mirabiliter difponente hec omnia fuo evenere Haroldo ut in ventre pregnantis ecclefie hominis ante tempora fecularia precogniti et fuis temporibus per hec omnia Deo nafcituri et perfecte placituri : offa compingerentur. Conceptus namque per devocionem fecundum interiorem hominem Deo . hiis exerciciis f. 7 b. crefcebat et augmentabatur formabatur et folidabatur : ut demum in parturicione egrediente pre dolore Rachelis anima fufciperet in eo Jacob pro Bennoni:[1] Benjamin. Qui enim matri fue videlicet angelice doloris et mortis filius vifus eft . patri Deo qui populum mente fuperbum crimine hifpidum variaque prodicione cruentum hoc eventu decreverat fupplantandum : filius dextere[2] mira ipfius permutacione effectus. Verum quia ubique fere terrarum celebri fermone vulgatum eft quemadmodum Edwardo fanctiffimo ad celefte tranflato in regno terreno fuccefferit Haroldus qualiter ejufdem favore de Norwagicis triumphaverit quamque magnanimiter quam celer et imparatus pre nimia mentis conftancia fupervenientibus Normannis occurrerit . ac cefis fociis ipfe quoque in hofte ceciderit : nos que poft hec per eum divinitus ac circa eum facta plerofque latere cognovimus : Domino favente

---

[1] In reference to Gen. xxxv. 18.
[2] H.M.; dextræ, G.

scribemus. Quorum alia a quodam venerabilis admodum vite anachorita nomine Sebrichto . qui viro beato pluribus dum adviveret ministravit annis . alia ab aliis eque fide dignissimis accepimus viris . qui nobis ea hec certitudine scribenda retulerunt: qua esse verissima indubitanter probaverunt. Porro que post felicem ipsius excessum a corpore celesti per eum virtute patrata : pagine asscribentur ab illis qui presentes cum fierent interfuerunt scripta nobisque transmissa sunt. Predictus autem vir Dei olim minister ejus et sequipeda devotissimus . ut ille de mundo recessit . et quia ad Deum abiit miraculorum indiciis patenter declaravit: ejus ferventer in bono emulabatur exemplum. Cupiens quippe quo ille pervenerat et ipse pervenire: studebat quam similius potuit sicut ille ambulaverat: et ipse ambulare. Igitur quod et Haroldum fuisse noverat peregrinacionis laborem amplexus natalis soli spontaneus exul . ut cujus sanctorum et domesticus Dei esse mereretur: efficitur. Nudus denique pedes a confinio recedit urbis Cestrensis ubi thesaurum quem devotus aliquot annis ibidem observant[1] parte in superni regis coronam sublata . partis reliquum humi defossum dimittebat : nudus eciam cupiditatis mundane progreditur. Sic nudus et expeditus crucem Dominicam in loco quo Dominicis aptata fuit membris aditurus: sepulcrum ejus gloriosum visitaturus . in loco ubi steterunt pedes ejus adoraturus . Angliam demum egreditur plurima nichilominus et alia sancta sanctorum limina ut fecerat Haroldus lacrimis rigaturus . linguas insuper quas

[1] H.M.; observarat, G.

non noverat auditurus . et tribulaciones pro Chrifto non modicas cum gaudio fubiturus . alienigenarum fines ingreditur. Poftremo voti faluberrimi compos effectus poft varios quos enumerare non vacat circuitus ad patrium ut Haroldus folum revertitur. Reverfus vero in villa quadam territorii Oxene- fordenfis Stantona[1] nomine fefe permanfurum recepit . receptum: inclufit. Inclufus plerifque ob fcelera claufis et incarceratis aufteriorem ufque ad mortem vitam duxit. Hinc religiofis quibufque venerabilis effectus et carus: a multis gracia edificacionis mutue: requiri folebat et defideranter adiri.

*De sequipeda id est ministro Haroldi incluso in villa de Stantone.*

Innotuerat enim devotiffimus Deo diftrictiffimus fibi affabilis cunctis . beneficus multis ; benevolus univerfis. Per hec et hujufmodi Chrifti cuicunque bonus odor effectus cum[2] in odore unguentorum ejus cuncti traherentur . me cum ceteris tanquam pufillum cum majoribus fimul rapuit . fibique arctius vinculo dileccionis aftrinxit. Quem adhuc vero tener . religionis profeffione tenellus . cum per internuncios utrobique graviores creberrime aliquociens[3] per memetipfum vifitaffem:[4] ad intima demum familiaritatis facraria ab ipfo admiffus fum. In quo tandem annis jam proveccior[5] adeo profeci: ut fecum de interioris hominis ftatu conferenti . vix quippiam fuorum michi fecretorum quod inftruccionis mee negotium expeteret: celare

---

[1] Stanton Harcourt, about five miles from Witney, G.

[2] H.M. ; quum, G. ; and fo always.

[3] H.M. ; aliquoties, G.

[4] Note in the margin of the MS. : "Auctor præfens fuit," in a handwriting of the fourteenth century.

[5] H.M.; provectior, G.

valuiffet. Qui cum rufticanus effet et totius eloquii alterius quam Anglici nefcius[1] . mirabilem tenebat . et amabilem de religionis fumma proque ydioma[2] fuo luculenter proferebat fentenciam . ut de meipfo aiebat . quod fencio dicam in paciencia et fpe falutis mee fummam puto confiftere. Subiciebat quanta oftendiffet fibi Dominus tribulaciones multas et magnas . quamque clementer converfus vivificaffet fe . et quam de abiffis[3] terre potenter reduxiffet fe. Interferebat et quanta paffus effet in corpore quanta in mente connumerans et diftinguens utriufque defectus hominis et varios affectus demonum affultus improbos . non parum quoque acerbos hominum infultus. Addebatque inter hec omnia jam jam paulo minus naufraganti fola mifero michi fpes in crucifixo pro anchora fuit . qua firmiter nifus omnia poft modicum quafi in fpumam et favillam evanuiffe vidi que paulo ante ipfa morte intolerabiliora duxi. Verumptamen[4] tales inquit ac tantas fuftinui afflicciones carnis . ex quo corpus miferum tanquam feram indomabilem hujus in quo five carceris inclufi anguftiis ut inexpertus quifque ferream materiam five lapideam vix umquam crederet tanta durare valuiffe.

Hec ille non jactabundus de fe ipfo et laboribus fuis pro Chrifto fet memorabat animandum me inter ipfa videlicet tyrocinii fpiritualis inexperta certamina trepidantem tanquam emeritus jam miles proprii fudoris familiari experimento ac roboran-

[1] Written twice in H. ; the firft word has a pen line drawn through it.
[2] H. ; ydioma[te], M. ; idiomate, G.
[3] H.M. ; abyffis, G.      [4] H.M. ; verumtamen, G.

dum talibus: eftimabat. Talia vero mente compunctus proferebat non eorum que pertuliffet erumpnam[1] deflens: fet illius quam ad erumpnarum[2] fuarum levamen percepiffet confolacionis et gracie fpiritualis memoriam : cum mira dulcedine eructans.

Hec de viri iftius vita et moribus non fuperflue ut eftimamus pagine videbantur inferenda . quatinus ex fanctitate alumpni liquidius docentur[3] quante perfeccionis culmine converfacio claruerit fui nutritoris. Hic de Haroldo mencionem faciens non aliter eum quam dominum fuum nominabat . ipfum profecto fe patronum habere in celo exultans quem preceptorem in mundo habuiffet. Per hunc igitur ut premiffum eft . et alios qui virum Dei viteque ipfius inftitutum variumque pro locis et temporibus ftatum agnoverant: ea que fecuntur comparata funt et vulgata. Horum nonnulli quod ipfe Haroldus ipfe[4] quondam in diademate gloriofus effet dum viveret nefcierunt converfacionis tamen illius teftes fuerunt . et quibus deguiffet in locis ex quo folitariam in Anglia duxit vitam plenius agnoverunt. Mundi namque gloriam cujus in feipfo ignobiles et lugubres exitus expertus fuiffet medullitus perhorcefcens[5] poftquam in terra olim fua vivere inftituit . nomen fibi novum ipfe impofuit . habitacionis quoque loca ne quis effet cui quolibet eventu proderetur non femel mutavit. Verum hec feriatim inferius profequemur :[6] nunc a digreffionis exceffu ad ordinem cepte narracionis ftilo currente accedamus.

[1] H.M.; ærumnam, G.    [2] H.M.; ærumnarum, G.
[3] H.; docentur, M.; doceatur, G.
[4] H.; the second *ipfe* omitted, M.G.
[5] H.M.; perhorrefcens, G.    [6] H.; perfequemur, M.G.

*Quod inter vulneratos feminecem inventum . et Wintoniam perductum mulier quedam Saracena biennio ibidem delitescentem sanaverit Haroldum . et quod pro contrahendis contra Normannos auxiliis Saxones Dacosque expecierit . nilque profecerit . v.*

ROSTRATO igitur ac superato in primo congressu a Normannis exercitu Anglorum Rex Haroldus plagis confossus innumeris inter mortuos . et ipse prosternitur. Nec poterant tamen quamlibet multa . quamlibet letalia vulnera vitam funditus viro adimere: quem pietas salvatoris ad vitam et victoriam felicius disposuit reparare. Recedentibus itaque a loco cedis hostilibus castris a mulierculis quas miseracio ad alliganda sauciorum vulnera illuc attraxerat: exanguis[1] jam et vix palpitans pugnator ille pridie potentissimus invenitur. Ab hiis[2] Samaritani erga eum vices implentur . ab hiis in vicinum tugurium . alligatis vulneribus suis deportatur. Inde a duobus ut fertur mediocribus viris quos francalanos sive agricolas[3] vocant agnitus .

---

[1] H.; exsanguis, M.G.       [2] H.; ab iis, M.G.

[3] Judging from the context, the *Francalanus* was probably the same as the *Franco homo* of Domesday, of whom Sir H.

et callide occultatus ad Wintonienfium deducitur civitatem. Hic biennio latebras in quodam cellario fovens a quadam muliere genere Saracena artis cirurgice peritiffima: curatus eft . et Altiffimi cooperante medicina: ad integerrimam perductus fanitatem. Qui viribus quoque receptis regie magnanimitatis confidenti:[1] quam animus nec in corporis ftrage omiferat: magnarum conatibus rerum credidit approbandam. Jam victoris fui jugo regni tocius nobilitas vulgufque colla fubmiferant . jam proceres pene cuncti aut perempti aut patria pulfi: avitos honores alienigenis parciendos ac poffidendos dimiferant.

Cernens itaque Haroldus fuorum cladem . hoftium felicitatem: corde ingemuit . et patrias magis quam proprias deplorans erumpnas[2]: aut commoriendum funditus aut fubveniendum civibus decernebat. Penalius enim ipfa quam vix effugiffet nece ducebat . fi nec fuis erepcioni fore temptaviffet miferrime viventibus: nec mifere peremptis ulcioni. Transfretavit igitur in Germaniam generis fui genitricem aditurus Saxoniam . gentis fue jam utrobique vulgatum miferabilem cafum cunctis ipfe miferandus deplorat . cognatos ad ferenda proprie ftirpi fuffragia inftanter folicitat. Allegat infortunium tam repentine cladis non viribus aut virtuti

*De transfretacione Haroldi in Germaniam. f. 9 b*

---

Ellis in his *Introduction*, ii. 112, gives a note, tending to fhew that thefe *francones homines* are entered as if attached to the manor, with the *villani* and *bordarii*. The *Francigena* (fee Ellis, *Introd.*, ii. 426) was probably one who could not fhew his right to be confidered an Englifhman.

[1] H.M.; confidentiam, G.
[2] H.M.; ærumnas, G.

hostium . non ignavie civium . non denique timiditati . non imbecillitati fue esse imputandum. Solam sibi in tali eventu animositatem fuisse periculo . que suarum conscia in rebus bellicis virium . et victoriarum . hostilem multitudinem cum paucissimo milite excepisset. Vincere enim assuetus et vinci nescius victum me ait credidissem . si paulo segnius novande[1] inimicis victoriam retulissem. Cesis namque favore divino a nobis cum rege suo Norwagicis qui regni nostri fines ab aquilone irruperant: exercitibus et ducibus nostris ad propria dimissis repente a regione australi supervenere Normanni. Quibus et ipse cum paucis repentinus occurrens non inferior viribus aut animis . sed numero minor compressus . tandem cecidi non victus cessi. Non incertam igitur victoriam de talibus confestim sumemus quos eventus non virtus hac vice superiores ostendit. Quorum in propriam[2] devocionem . et sua insolencia . et tocius nobis premeditate congressionis modus et exacerbate multitudinis copiosa solacia exhibebunt. Hiis et hujusmodi Saxones talibus quoque Dacos quos nichilominus sollicite adivit pro expugnandis secum regni sui invasoribus interpellat. Quorum studia ut vidit in diversa niti in que[3] sua minus percurrere vota primo quidem graviter anxie mentis fluctibus estuare cepit . vehementerque addici. In hoc quippe ut erat sagacissimus securitati sue rex jam Anglorum et Normannorum dux caute prorsus

---

[1] H.M.; novam de, G.
[2] H.; promptu, G.; perpetu[am], M.
[3] H.; inque, M.G.

follerterque profpexerat ut miffa legacione regis gentifque Dacorum aliarum eciam finitimarum nacionum amicicias fibi abftringere [1] . et graciam conciliare feftinaret.

[1] H.M.; adftringere, G.

*Quod in se tandem idem reversus, intellexit[1] Deum sibi in via mundi adversari unde Christi se conformans cruci ut hostem melius triumpharet antiquum gaudet se ab hominibus fuisse superatum . vj.*

ANDEM vero in se reversus Haroldus et quasi a fantastico quo diucius sompnio sibi redditus ad cor suum totus convertitur. Intelligit vel sero obsistentem sibi in via hac qua inaniter ambulabat Deum . suique fuisse angeli quem intus exteriusque in se sue tam pertinaciter cedentem pertulisset gladium. Apertisque mentis sue oculis aliud de cetero sibi genus eligendum videt preliorum alia requirenda presidia. Respexerat enim oculo jam propicio crucifixus rex regis dejecti labores et longos cruciatus . nec ulterius paciebatur peculiarem vexilli sui cultorem tanti meroris abysso demergi involvi laberinto.[2] Respexerat sane . lapsum crimine . et lapsum a dignitate quo respiciente lapsus cadunt: et lapsi resurgunt. Respexerat denique ut fletu lapsus culpam dilueret . spem vero et studium regnandi non deponeret sed mutaret. Cepit igitur

---

[1] H.; intellexerit, M.G.      [2] H.M.; labyrintho, G.

lapsus videre et deflere sub aspectu cuncta cernentis criminum suorum et errorum lapsus cepit regni longe felicioris faciliorem multo viam agnoscere. et copiam presentire. Sedet animo crucis quam amaverat imitatorem esse tollere quotidie crucem suam venire post crucifixum: et ipsum sequi. Nec vero a mente excidit quia ut ad hec idoneus fieri possit se ipsum in primis abnegare necesse sit. Quod nichilominus ut possit eundem ipsum sibi in exemplum proponit et adjutorem assumit. qui cum in forma Dei esset seipsum formam servi accipiens exinanivit. Intuetur jam qualiter Dominus mundi mundanum cum esset in mundo sprevit imperium. qui et quesitus in regem: fugerit. et milibus obsequencium turbis solitarie orationis secessum pretulerit. Reminiscitur datam huic per passionis dure et mortis dire supplicium omnem in celo et in terra potestatem. Previdet ab omni carne huic tandem occurrendum. donandum ab eo omnem hominem regno vel supplicio meminit sempiterno. Scit quidem[1] si eatur ad committendum bellum cum eo ipse cum decem milibus sibi occurrenti obvius cum viginti milibus veniat cujus adventus improvisus cujus dispar apparatus. quam[2] latenter invadit tam potenter improvidum quemque et imparatum nonnunquam exterminat et extinguit.

Posthabito igitur inani temporalis regni studio abjecto terrene concertacionis exiciali proposito. Ad hunc regem adhuc longe agentem legationem mittere ab eo que vere pacis sunt tota proponit intencione postulare. Cujus tamen iram suis ut

[1] Quoniam, G.; qm, H.; quantum, M.  [2] H.; quem, M.G.

timebat offenfis cumulatam ne fua forte fola legacio minus fufficeret delinire: inquirendos cenfuit et quibus poffet obfequiis inquirendos . et fue legacionis congruos adjutores et ydoneos apud iratum regem interventores . cujus de cetero folius gratiam probavit et gloriam ambiendam. Mutatur itaque in Haroldo hominis repente exterioris habitus . et interioris affectus. Fulcit quam armare confuevit manum . curtata in baculum hafta . pro clipeo: pera collo appenditur . filtro vertex adumbratur : quem munire galea . ornare diadema folebat. Pedes et tybie pro fandaliis et ocreis vel nudantur funditus vel femicinciis obvolvuntur. Ut autem et reliqua breviter explicemus: omnis armatura fortis . totus potentis ornatus vel abdicatur penitus . aut in abjeccionem transfertur : et penitentis penam. Nam humeris lacertis . lumbis et lateri: lorica folum . folita non adimitur . fed proprius admovetur. Abftracta[1] fiquidem et abjecta interula: nude carni calibis duricies copulatur. Sic vigilans non armatus fed incarceratus incedit ferro . fic dormientem non thorus excipit . fed thorax includit. Et mira plane exterius affumpta mutacio ifta. Jocundum fane et angelis et omnibus fanctis fpectaculum . circa tantum et talem virum . talis ac tanta permutacio rerum . verum multo jocundius intra ipfum fibimet exhibebat interius arbiter Deus . creans et formans in eo pro tenebris lucem . et univerfum ftratum ejus mirabiliter verfans. Vere inquam mutacio hec: non cujufcunque fed dextere excelfi ubi crudelitas . et feritas mitefcit in cle-

---

[1] G. ; abftincta, M. ; abftincta, altered to abftracta, H.

menciam et lenitatem . contrahitur elatio: in humilitatem . Set quis mutacionis adeo felicis universa commemoret? Ut innumera vel[1] paucis includam . hac mutacione concupiscencia carnis . et mundi in horum versa contemptum et odium: desiderio cessit et amori celestium.

Sic sic operante dextera excelsi rex transit in militem et militem quidem Christi: plus jam contempto quam prius cupito regno mundi. Transit rex in militem efficitur rex miles . ut ita efficiatur miles rex, et rex simul ac miles transeat [in regem. f. 11. Illi enim militare aggreditur miles iste cui militare regnare est . et regnare quidem in presenti: in futuro conregnare. Illud vero conregnare multo felicius quam istud regnare est quod tamen regnare mundo et mundi regno sublimius et majus est. Militando quidem regnat et regnando militat . donec mutet mansuris mutabilia miles Christi et absorbeatur mors in victoriam . et bellum vertatur in tropheum.[2] Tunc rex transibit in regem militans in triumphantem sollicitus in securum moribundus in semper victurum. Interea innovato rege innovato et milite . regnum novum in Haroldo cum innovata successit milicia: ipsius quoque cum singulis suis sensibus et membris in novos reflorescit usus mundi cordis et corporis substancia tota. In fame et siti in frigore et nuditate in orationibus in vigiliis in contumeliis[3] et injuriis . in omni denique labore et erumpna maceratur caro roboratur

[1] H. ; vel, omitted, M.G. This is a clear instance of Giles copying Michel instead of reading the M.S.
[2] H.M. ; tropæum, G.   [3] H.M. ; contumelis, G.

fpiritus: anima delectatur. Quatitur fufpiriis pectus hanelum[1]. quod prius tumidum: fpirabat cedis minas intonabat. Rorant lumina imbre lacrimarum. Fulmineum quiddam indignantis animi nutu in emulos confueta vibrare. Nil jam elatum cervicofum nichil aut truculentum os fupercilia. et cervix pretendebant. Modeftia inceffum regit pietas animum. affectus: puritas fibi defendit. Interiores quoque motus et exteriores: honeftas informat. fanctitas in fuas partes omnia ejus affumit. Videtur jam fibi Haroldus folito felicius imperare. regnare fublimius tucius et utilius militare. Gaudet fe ab hominibus victum. dum mundum dum feipfum vincendo: victus quoque melius de Diabolo didicit triumphare.

[1] H.; Quantis s. p. anhelat, M.; q. s. p. anhelum, G.

*Quod pro expetendis sanctorum suffragiis longum inierit peregrinacionem et quod antequam regnum habuisset sanctorum limina apostolorum adierit . vij.*

NSTRUCTUS vero ab[1] unccione que jam illum docebat de omnibus celestis quem invenerat thesaurum desiderii ne prede pateat inepte publicatus . caucius sentit abscondendum. Nam et ovis primo genita seu bovis nec apta sciebat aratris . nec tondenda . quin et poma que germinant: legis sanccione immunda decerni. Hujusmodi ergo a Spiritu Sancto edoctus oraculis, omnes qui sibi usque ad id temporis adhesisse visi sunt: amicos f. 11. b. relinquid . necessarios deserit . ab universis demum qui ipsum noverant: clam recedit. Adit populos antea ignotos . requirit non ignotos . sed olim quidem dileccione precognitos jam devocionis affectu arctius complexos: longe lateque patronos. Abiit igitur in regionem longinquam[2] vir iste nunc vere nobilis . loca invisere sacra sanctorum in suis ubique sedibus . aut edibus veneraturus reliquias . regnum Dei quod intra se jam tenebat corum suf-

---

[1] H.M. ; omitted, G.   [2] H.G. ; lo[n]ginquam, G.

fragiis plenius et perfeccius accipere . et in fuam demum patriam reverti. Adierat quidem antea nondum videlicet Anglorum confecutus regnum fummorum limina Chrifti apoftolorum devocionis plane inftinctu . et fanctarum ab urbe reliquiarum ad fua pocius reportandi quam in urbe adorandi obtentu. Ferventiffimo namque ftudio facras colligere fategerat reliquias[1] ab illo prefertim tempore quo Sancte Crucis edificare apud Waltham ut predictum eft ecclefiam cepit: et ditare. Unde accidit ut votis precum folutis tum prece tum precio varioque ingenio innumeris fanctorum pignorum opibus adquifitis magnificorum quoque martyrum [2]

[1] For a long lift of thefe relics fee MS. Harl. 3776, f. 31. The chapter treating of them commences with a fhort poem:

"Hoc facrum pondus fibi confervavit Haroldus
Scilicet iftarum thefaurus reliquiarum.
Quas tulit ignotis a partibus atque remotis.
Unde crucis fancte : fe premuniret in ede."

[2] The Virgin martyrs Chryfanthus and Daria are celebrated in the Calendar on the 25th October. According to Alban Butler (vol. x., p. 502) Chryfanthus and Daria were ftrangers who came to Rome from the Eaft in the third century, the firft from Alexandria, the fecond from Athens. Chryfanthus, after having efpoufed Daria, perfuaded her to prefer a ftate of perpetual virginity to that of marriage, that they might more eafily with perfect purity of heart trample the world under their feet, and accomplifh the folemn confecration they had made of themfelves to Chrift in their baptifm. Their martyrdom probably took place during the perfecution of Valerian, A.D. 237. They were interred on the Salarian way, their remains being found in the reign of Conftantine the Great. This part of the Catacombs was long known by the name of the Cemetery of SS. Chryfanthus and Daria. Their tomb was decorated by Pope Damafus, their remains tranflated by Pope Stephen VI. in A.D. 866, part into the Lateran bafilica, and part into the Church of the Twelve Apoftles. This, at leaft, is true of the relics of their companions who had

Crisanti et Darie rediens ad propria beata simul ossa visus sit asportasse a Roma. Verum tanti predam thesauri tandem sibi prereptam Romani sencientes et id non eque ferentes: jam abeuntem . jam longius abscedentem diete jam tercie seu quarte emenso itinere pium consecuti predonem gressum sistere cogunt. Nec enim reniti aut viribus vel fuga erumpere indigenarum multitudo paucos sinebat peregrinos. Quid multa? Tenetur . arctatur . conviciis urgetur Haroldus. Quodque hiis egrius tulit . pristinis possessoribus minus[1] prout asserebant legittime conquisitas: reddere compellitur inestimabilis precii margaritas. Predictorum igitur Christi testium in divinis non suffragiis violencia Romanorum spoliatus . cetera non minus preciosissima Rome obiterve[2] adquisita . in ecclesia sepius memorata patrie redditus secum attulit reverentissime conservanda. Devocionis vero illius et Nota. cautele . vigilanciam in adquirendis et reservandis sanctorum reliquiis si quem plenius nosse juvat: prenotatum de invencione crucis Waltamensis superius tractatum studiose revolvat. Nos enim f. 12. que a veteribus scripta sunt intermittentes: novum nostrum novo stili officio prosequemur ut cepimus Christo ducente peregrinum. Quem et si multas perlustrantem orbis Christiani provincias . totque

---

been walled up at their tomb. The remains of SS. Chrysanthus and Daria had been translated to the Abbey of Prom in the diocese of Triers in A.D. 842, by gift of Pope Sergius II. In A.D. 844 they were removed to the Abbey of St. Avol or St. Navor in the diocese of Metz, according to Mabillon, *Sæc. iv. Bened.* p. 611.

[1] H. ; omitted, M.G.    [2] G. ; ob iter ve, H.M.

tam falubriter in tali perluftracione tempora confumentem nec locis fingulis nec diebus comitari valemus queve egerit aut pertulerit in peregrinacione longiffima fingillatim noffe ac referre: faltem a finibus noftris elongatum jam diucius profecuti . ad nos quoque denuo remeanti alacrius occurramus. Comitantem vero . et deducentem nullifque aliquando temporibus aut locis ipfum relinquentem . Dominum magnifice collaudemus benedicentes in Domino pariter et famulum fuum: venientem equidem in nomine Domini.

*Ammiracio* [1] *fcriptoris cum exclamacione brevi fuper benignitate Dei qua fit ut eciam peccata electorum ipfis cooperentur in bonum* . . *viij.*

NTERIM autem in hoc nomine illo ambulante . illius anima per multarum cum fponfa circuicionem platearum quefitum et inventum tenente fponfum . ipfius jam fpiritum in Deo falutari fuo exultantem gratulabunda cum pfalmifta audire michi videor voce canentem . "Convertere [2] . anima mea . in requiem tuam: quia Dominus benefecit tibi." Hic vero precordis leticia benefici Domini circa fervum fuum admirando magnalia: exclamare libet. O larga pietas et mira benignitas fpiritus tui O virtus et fapientia eterni Patris coeterne fili O dulcis O bone Jefu. O ineftimabilem et inveftigabilem confiliorum tuorum altitudinem . Vere cogitaciones cordis tui avertere nemo poteft. O quam vera fenfit de te que alloquens te. "Si [3] decreveris" ait . "falvare nos: continuo liberabimur." Quam fidelis quamque accepcione dignus fermo .

---

[1] The text of this chapter is omitted by Michel, who ftates, "In quo hiftoriæ materiam minime reperies."
[2] Pfalm. cxiv. 7.   [3] Cf. Efth. xiii. 9.

fidenter prolatus ad apostolo tuo. "Scimus" inquit "quoniam diligentibus[1] Deum: omnia cooperantur in bonum." Benedictum sit cum patre coeterno . et Spiritu coevo nomen glorie tue sanctum . qui cum iratus fueris misericordiam facis et ut asserit mulier sancta: omnia peccata hominum in tribulacione dimittis. Et quidem omnia hec vera esse et in hunc modum innumera . que passim leguntur in literis sacris de te super hiis que perficis et exhibes diligentibus te in uno demonstrasti[2] tuo hoc dilecto dilectore. Quam evidens nobis argumentum quam prelucidum in uno homine isto suavitatis simul et fortitudinis tue speculum condidisti O sapientia que ex ore Altissimi prodidisti attingens a fine usque ad finem fortiter et disponens omnia suaviter. Ab hiis fontibus suavitatis et fortitudinis illi duo rivi procedunt gratie et severitatis seu clemencie et districcionis quibus debriata superficies terre sanctorum eversis zizanniis[3] semen producit in fructum vite eterne. Quante enim serenitatis pariter et gratie fuit quod sicut multi putant propter iniquitatem corripuisti quidem sed in eternum non projecisti hominem istum . corripiens et corrigens caucioremque sibi . tibi devociorem ex ipsa quoque iniquitate exhibens eum. Quanta suavitate quantaque fortitudine usus es circa eum tam valide de manu mortis eripiens illum vitam corporis ejus nec jaculis nec gladiis sibi permittens auferri . vitam vero anime etiam[4] peccato ut dicitur ablatam restituens et reformans ei? Hinc et ipsius injusticia inventa

[1] Rom. viii. 28.  [2] H.; demonstrati, G.
[3] H.; zizaniis, G.  [4] H.; et, G.

eſt habundare in gloriam tuam . quandoquidem ex multa magnitudine et magna multitudine dulcedinis benignitatis tue ubi habundavit iniquitas ſua ſuperhabundavit in eo gratia tua . ut eo impenſius diligeret te . quo plenius indulgenciam conſequeretur a te. Itaque clareſceret quia diligenti te cooperantur in bonum non aliqua ſed omnia dum quod in malum ſemper eſt: ei cooperatur in bonum eternum[1] . ſuum videlicet et tantum peccatum.

[1] H.; non æternum, G.

*Quod de peccato Haroldi multa dicuntur a multis et de quercu secus Rothomagum sub qua juraverat quæ corticem exuta manet usque in præsens . . . . . . . ix.*

E quo nimirum ipsius peccato quia multi multa loquuntur . loqui debemus vel pauca et nos: et quid de eo senciant qui vel exaggerare vel qui attenuare illud familiare habent in medium proferre. Nam ipsum non qualemcumque[1] sed immanissimum pat[r]asse[2] peccatum plerique accusant in tantum ut huic ejus enormi peccato Anglice libertatis ruinam estiment imputandam. Assumpsisse enim in vanum asseritur nomen Domini Dei sui adeo ut perjurio illud polluere non timeret cujus piaculi crimen prodigio mirabili divinitus quoque astruunt denotari. Quercus enim proceritatis magne. multeque olim pulchritudinis sicut hodie quoque cernentibus demonstratur sub qua jurisjurandi sacramentum duci Normannorum prestitit: mox ut illud regnum quod ei servandum juraverat .

---

[1] H.M.; qualecumque, G.
[2] Patasse, H.; pat[r]asse, M.; patrasse, G.

usurpando infregit: virore deposito defluentibus foliis corticem quod dictu mirum est repente exuisse perhibetur. Res digna spectaculo quod lignum multis condensisque frondibus paulo ante speciosum non segnius quam hedera,[1] ione[2] . quam oliva alterius prophete radicitus exaruit albique facti sunt rami ejus. Auget miraculum subditi marcoris: perpetuitas invicti roboris arboris exsiccate quod frequenter cum plurimis et ipsi mirati sumus. Quis enim non obstupescat vaste magnitudinis robor . ramusculis etiam minutis non imminutum sed undique inconfractum ab imis radicibus usque ad summitatem frondium omni velamento corticis spoliatum . tot jam seculis nec etate cessisse . nec carie tabuisse . nec ventorum turbine impactum . nec imbrium inundacione infusum . putruisse . vel saltem nutasse? Quo signo in anni circiter centesimi quadragesimi spacium[3] cum arborem vidimus jam porrecto . infandi scelus perjurii vicinorum loco Rothomagus jactuabat . celitus infamari. Modico namque intervallo ab urbe ipsa distat arbor infausta ameno imminens saltui qui strate non multum abjacet a ponte Sequane ad Grandimontenses[4] eremitas[5] sese protendenti. Omine tam

[1] Jonah iv. 6, 7, 9, 10.    [2] H.M.; Ionæ, G.
[3] If this be taken to signify that the author beheld the withered tree after a lapse of 140 years from the occurrence, we arrive at a date certainly prior to A.D. 1206, the seventh and eighth regnal year of King John.
[4] "Anno 1156 Henricus II. prioratum ordinis Grandimontensis fundavit in Silva Roboreti, quem paulo post in vivarium suum prope Rotomagum transtulit ad sinistram fluminis Sequanæ ripam ; unde locus ille nomen sumsit beatæ Mariæ de Vivario." *Gallia Christiana*, xi. 47. c.
[5] " La première vie des religieux de Grandmont, fut celle

invifo Londonias primum fibi prefumpfiffe fertur Rothomagus fubjugandas. Nec alio magis aufpicio tota fimul Neuftria egentis et avare domine compendiis prodigas Anglorum opes ancillari poffe: docta eft non defperare. Hiis adicitur[1] ab illis qui Haroldum jam vere victorem linguis adhuc infectantur . illius poft modum ac poft modicum confecuta quam facilis tam et crudelis dejeccio qua ut inopinate regnum amifit. Sic infufpicabiliter vitam vix confervando necem evafit.

des ermites, fi l'on en croit l'opinion commune, différente de celle du père Mabillon," etc.—Richard et Giraud, *Biblioth. Sacr.*, xii. 262.

[1] H.M.; adjicitur, G.

*Satisfaccio quorumdam pro Haroldo qua eum de perjurio excusantes Domino favente et Sancto connivente Edwardo ipsum regnasse affirmant et de visione abbatis Elfini qua victorem Norwagicorum ipsum fore prenunciavit sanctus Edwardus . x.*

DIVERSO nonnulli ex fine ipsius . et creberrime eciam antea interlucentibus circa eum superni favoris indiciis viri Deo dilecti factum mecientes . tam jurisjurandi minus observati . quam regni quoque rite suscepti : nituntur inducere rationem . Quod enim rem ut ex postfacto inquiunt manifestum f. 13 b. est universe procul dubio genti sue exicialem si observaretur juravit: tam sue voluntati adversum quam suorum saluti contrarium fuit. Juravit Nota de juramento Haroldi. tamen metu constrictus qui in virum constantem et continuo mori vel perpetuo incarcerari renuentem non immerito caderet. Nec vero alius a tantis angustiis patebat exitus: in terra aliena in manu potestatis tante concluso . fragilitati ergo mortali que vitam nisi in vita . vix exuit morem gerens et consilio qualiumcunque in tali tempore presencium amicorum : exortum[1] prestitit juramentum in quo

[1] H.M. ; extortum, G.

## Vita Haroldi Regis.

et leges mundane et divini canones variis vite hujus neceffitatibus condefcendiffe . non ignorantur. De jure extorquentis hujufmodi facramentum . alii ut libuerit difputabunt. Licuit vero ut manifeftum eft fic elicitum . fi tamen quod nemo diffitetur eciam illicitum fuiffet : non implere juramentum. Hac vero quia alias nequivit de medio fe tenentium Haroldus exiit Normannorum. Qui fuis demum redditus quid pertulerit . quid egerit : cunctis palam exponit. Exponentem ut audit : univerfitas in iram excandefcit . initam mediante facramento paccionem improbat ne obfervetur . vehementer reclamat. Abfit inquiunt abfit ut ferviamus Normannis! Abfit ut faftus Normanici jugo barbarico : nobilitatis Anglice urbana libertas nullatenus fubfternatur! Quid multa?

Conclamant omnes, fedet hec fentencia cunctis.

Pofthabitoque juramenti quod nullum effe credebatur periculo : Haroldus demum unanimi omnium confilio fublimatur in regem. Quod preter divinitatis nutum minime accidiffe : celitus poft in brevi fuerat declaratum . cum enim rex Norwagenfis[1] claffe advectus numerofa intraffet Angliam aggreffufque Eboracenfem provinciam cede et incendiis obvia queque vaftaret illique rex novus coacto exercitu feftinaret occurrere tybie fubito unius vehementiffimo cepit dolore conftringi. Qui ex fuo tali compede plus fubditorum difcrimini quam fuo congemifcens dolori noctem pene totam

*Nota de infirmitate tybie.*

*f. 14.*

---

[1] For account of this invafion and its refult, fee the Anglo-Saxon Chronicle, *ad annum* 1066.

suspiriis et precibus agentes insompnem familiarem sancte crucis[1] expecierat subvencionem. In ipsa vero nocte astititit in visione servo Domini Elfino[2] abbati Ramesiensi sanctus et vigil propugnator suorum rex Edwardus predecessor viri merentis et afflicti exponens . abbati regis utrumque et corporis scilicet et cordis incommodum cogitaciones insuper illius in cubili suo ei manifestans . mittensque eum et dicens ei. "Surgens vade et annunciabis regi vestro ex me quia et presentis sui doloris medelam et imminentis belli me interveniente Deus ei concessit victoriam. Sit ei cogitacionum cordis sui revelatio consequende incontinenti divinitus signum medicine sit et revelacionis insolite argumentum: capessende victorie presagium indubitatum." Rex itaque ut paucis utamur divinis curatur beneficiis exhilaratur oraculis. Hostes fidenter aggressus facile vincit . quia non . suis sed illius viribus superavit . qui sanat contritos corde et alligat contritiones eorum . deiciens[3] gladio diligentium se hostes suorum. Colligitur ergo racione non improbabili suadente . quia sanctissimo predecessore

[1] H.M.; carcis, G.

[2] This Abbot Elfinus is the Alfwynus or Aylwynus of Dugdale, who places him from A.D. 1043-1079. The Anglo-Saxon chronicle mentions him as Ælfwine in A.D. 1046 or 1048. He occurs in several charters in Kemble's *Codex* as Alwinus (No. 809), Ælfwinus (Nos. 853, 904, 919), Ælfwine (No. 853), Ælfwin (No. 904), and Ælfwyne (No. 904). The French metrical poem printed by Rev. Mr. Luard among the "Master of the Rolls Series" (No. 3), p. 143, says:

"Une abés fu de Ramseie,
Ki *Alexe* ont nun, de seinte vie,
E li aparut seint Aedward," etc.

[3] H.M.; dejiciens, G.

fuo connivente—Deo quam maxime[1] difponente regnum fuerit affecutus quod fancti et patrocinio munitus et oraculo premonitus divino aftipulante fuffragio de hofte fuperbo tam meruit triumphaliter liberare.

[1] Thefe words repeated by error of the fcribe, and afterwards their firft introduction into the text fcored through with the pen.

*De cruce sancta admirabilis quorumdam relacio .
que Regi Haroldo festinanti ad prelium . caput per-
bibetur inclinasse et alia quedam satis de ipsa cruce
stupenda certissime approbata*[1] . . . *xj.*

UI adhuc non folum hiis racionibus et fignis defenfa eft legittima fceptri- gere poteftatis adepcio . et ejufdem favorabilis execucio comprobatur. Novo enim et feculis omnibus inaudito Sal- vatoris clemencia fuum dignata eft peculiarem fervum figno iterum fublimius infignire quo unius fimul tam privilegiati titulo miraculi et fuum erga devotum regem et favorem oftenderet et amorem . et illius contra probra infamancium perenniter defenfaret honorem. Res ubique prope modum vulgata eft . oculifque ad hoc ufque tempus fubjecta que accidit. Revertens fiquidem a cede hoftium rex fortiffimus: et novis qui fuper- venerant feftinus occurrens inimicis . dilectam fibi ecclefiam nulla patitur feftinacionis inftancia pre- terire. Divertit igitur devotus, ad ipfam ingreditur, profternitur . et liquefactis intimis[2] precordiorum

[1] See MS. Harl. 3776, f. 54. "De eleccione et coronacione et de inclinacione capitis Sancte crucis."
[2] H., internis, M.G.

medullis: Crucem fanctam adorat . vota graciarum pro optento[1] tropheo[2] exaggerat pro optinendo fi placeat fumme majeftati: preces fuppliciter ingeminat. Oracione poftremo completa: imminentis belli eventu cuncta moderantis arbitrio fideli devocione attencius delegato feipfum victoriofiffimo figno commendans cum receffurus jam demiffo vertice et prono corpore cruci facrofancte valefacturus de more inclinaret fe: inclinavit pariter fe vultus ymaginis[3] crucifixe. Terruit nimirum et exhilaravit quofdam aftancium mirabile . et favorabile opus Salvatoris. Quid enim favorabilius vel cogitari potuit quam ut rex feculorum immortalis invifibilis vifibiliter refalutare videretur regem mortalium miferorum falutantem fe . et fibi humiliter caput inclinanti caput fibi faxee ymaginis quam dignanter tam et potenter inclinare? Quam nichilominus et terribile infirmitati humane fuit tam infolita videre ut contra naturam faxum flecteretur et quod fupra naturam eft Deus in fua ymagine homini inclinare cerneretur! De hoc vero quid dicemus quod ubi ars humana nec tenuem valuit divine ymaginis perforare palmam . ibi ymago ipfa flexiffe vifa eft cervicem corpulentam? Sudat homo artifex et cruorem elicit: foramen vero in manu lapideum efficit.[4] Orat homo in brevi defiturus effe rex . et collum lapideum quod manu hominis et fi aliquatenus foraretur nullatenus tamen flecteretur . flectitur

---

[1] H.; obtenti, M.; obftento, G.
[2] H.M.; tropeo, G.
[3] H.M.; imaginis, G.; and fimilarly throughout in cafes of this word.        [4] H.; [non] efficit, M.G.

repente nec frangitur . inclinatur sed a tocius integritate subjecti corporis vel annexi capitis nec tenuissima rima mediante dissipatur. Nec in simplici tantum materia tale . et tantum effulsit miraculum. Nam quod lapis interius latens hec et argentum exterius ambiens duplicato videlicet prodigio pertulit pariter et ostendit. Ipsa nempe illius ymago de quo scriptum est . *Suxerunt*[1] *mel de petra oleumque de saxo durissimo* . materia quidem petrina . immo et saxea est . qualitate durissima : circa humeros collum et lacertos spissa . et ut ita dicatur corpulenta.

Hec revelacione divina in montis cujusdam vertice sub terra fuit reperta . nec sciri hactenus potuit quomodo vel a quo sculpta sit vel ibidem reposita et occultata. Perducta quoque est celesti regimine ad locum sepius nominatum . quo hec contigisse perhibentur bobus nimirum carrum cui imposita fuit ad transferendum eam per centum viginti circiter miliaria[2] illuc directe pergentibus nec aliorsum a cepto itinere declinari sinentibus. Ibi laminis argenteis vestita . et patibulo eminenti annexa nec affixa fuit. Nec enim vel tantillum artificii in sese admisit humani . ut foramina quibus clavi de more induci valuissent : in ea ullatenus homo facere potuisset. Nec enim istud intemptatum[3] fuit . Verum palma dextere illius ferreo vix instrumento aliquantulum superficie tenus terebrata molliciem habuisse inventa est . unde emisit sanguinem . sed duriciem non amisit qua

---

[1] Deut. xxxii. 13.   [2] H.M.; milliaria, G.
[3] H.M.; intentatum, G.

repulit acutissimam celtem vel tarincam. Prestitit hoc ymaginis[1] sue dextere[2] Domini dextera . que ut psalmista[3] . cecinit fecit virtutem . unde et materiali huic dextere que ibidem subnectitur congrue adaptatur . ut ipsa tot signis insignita tot prodigiis sublimata . rebus pocius quam sermonibus dicere intelligatur . *Dextera[4] Domini exaltavit me dextera Domini fecit virtutem.* Hec vero omnia nunc iccirco retulimus ut clarefceret audientibus multiplicitas Dominice virtutis . quam in tali fecit inclinacione sancti capitis sacrosancte ymaginis . ut enim prefati sumus tam in argentea quam in lapidea effulsit materia Dominice dignacionis pariter et virtutis opus hoc admirabile in oculis nostris quod juxta cornu altaris . ubi hoc gestum est cotidie inspicimus. Nec enim vel lapis crepuit vel lamina scissuram sensit seu rugam contraxit . cum a parte colli racione inclinacionis tante solito amplius tenderetur . et e regione gutturis et faucium non minori proporcione plicari cerneretur. Nec vero parva fuit primarie disposicionis immutacio . ubi mentum ymaginis quod eminuisse olim accepimus . nunc ad pectus usque demissum ei velut infedisse ex premissa ut dictum est inclinacione videmus.

[1] H.M.; imaginis, G.
[2] H.M.; dextra, G.; and so always in cases of this word.
[3] Psa., H.; pura, M.; psalmista, G.
[4] Psalm. cxvii. 16.

*Diverforum*[1] *diverfa interpretacio fuper prediƐtis fignis crucis fe inclinantis et quercus arefaƐte: et quod Haroldus feipfum judicando judicium prevenerit divinum et non formidet humanum* . . *xii.* f. 15 b.

OC quoque tante pietatis opus quam dulce et propicium tunc prefentibus vifum eft omen portendiffe tam infauftum et crudele pofterorum nonnulli pretendiffe dixerunt. Triumphato namque in brevi poft hec cum fuis rege eorum: fubjeccionem Anglorum lamentabilemque depreffionem regni inclinacionem iftam prefignaffe plurimi eftimabant. Ceterum quibus rei gefte ordinem . et regis devoti erga crucem precedens pariterque fubfequens meritum attendentibus . longe verifimilior meritoque benignior in opere tam divino occurrit interpretacio. Deus enim qui merita fupplicum femper excedit et vota . fupplices fuos fupra quam petunt et intelligunt: exaudire jugiter confuevit. Unde multociens[2] quos clemencius exaudit ad falutem . durius exaudit ad voluntatem.

[1] This chapter omitted, M., with the following note: "Hoc capitulum omifimus ut longum et infulfum valde."

[2] H.; multoties, G.

Nam ad voluntatem contra eorum falutem: fuos exaudit folum inimicos. Nec eft neceffe de quibufcunque electis aut reprobis utriufque exaudicionis exempla memorando: fermonem in longum protrahere. Sufficit reproborum principem confiderare fanctum virum Job ad temptandum petiffe. et femel et iterum accepiffe. ficque ad dampnacionis fue cumulum exauditum effe. Satis fit e diverfo ipfum electorum omnium caput meminiffe paffionis imminente aculeo calicis tranflacionem petife nec optinuiffe fue tamen voluntatis nutum evidencius expreffiffe fet patris beneplacito ipfam fubjeciffe immo et ipfam penitus abjeciffe.[1] Non inquit mea voluntas fet tua fiat. Deus enim in tali voluntate proprio filio non pepercit pro omnibus nobis tradens illum. ut cum de torrente in via bibiffet propterea exaltaret caput: quod in cruce quum bibiffet continuo inclinavit. Premiffe tamen confummacionis diccio: hoftis humani generis denunciata deviccio fuit. Qua denunciacione promulgata caput inclinavit in pace dormiens. poft follicitudinis bellice longas vigilias. et poft fanguinei fudoris agonem. in pace in id ipfum fuaviter requiefcens. Hec vero increduli: in contrarium converterunt. Quando vero triumphum de inimicis confummavit. tunc fe regem victorem livor devictus viciffe credebat. Ipfe autem quid egiffet non incertus, caput invictum, et donec vinceret femper erectum in fompnum tam plene fecurus inclinavit. Patet jam quam peculiari figno fideli adoratori fuo victoriam meliorem quam ceteri

---

[1] Immo . . . abjeciffe, H.; omitted, G.

peterent aut intelligerent . caput inclinando rex
regi se ostenderit concessisse. Ne enim prevaleret
erronea victorum contra sui victorem existimacio:
et crederetur regnum amisisse qui Judeorum rex
dicebatur esse accessit presidis litteris indita opinionis temerarie improbacio . capiti jam inclinato:
titulo suppofito. Erat enim scriptum in eo:
*Jesus*[1] *Nazarenus rex Judeorum.* Permansit enim
vere rex . cui plebs impia quia regnum invidit ut
ejus caput inclinaret: et ipsum occidit. At ille
pariter et caput inclinavit et sibi regni potenciam
vendicavit quam se plenius accepisse convescens,
caput in tantum inclinatum super omnes celos
exaltavit. Nemo igitur existimet nomen regium
seu regiam regi cui[2] tale signum prestitum est a
rege regum omnium . dignitatem deperisse: vel
quia sibi in sua ymagine inclinari dignatus est, vel
quia visibiliter triumphare de hostibus imminenti-
bus ab eodem eidem permissum non est. Si vero
et ad regnum cujus sibi temporalis administracio
divinitus collata prius est et posterius ablata . presagium tam insolite virtutis duxerit quis exten-
dendum Anglice felicitatis depressionem necnon
et libertatis tam laice quam ecclesiastice non abnui-
mus consignificari insulanis extunc[3] satis expertam
dejectionem. Verumptamen ex hoc servi sui prerogative crux sancta prejudicari non patitur . quia
et quiddam aliud id quod pro eo specialiter egit .
universaliter signare concedit. Ipsius nempe gemi-
tibus pulsata et lacrimis . obsequiis insuper magnifice honorata: pro gratis officiis votiva ei non

[1] John xix. 19. [2] Cui, H.; omitted, G. [3] H.; ex tunc, G.

autem invisa rependere . debuit vel pronunciare.
Set neque transitoria et caduca immo stancia bona
et eterna piis prestat et promittit cultoribus eter-
nus . et invariabilis Deus pro suis laboribus vel
obsequiis. Annuit ergo dedit et concessit rex regi
quod peciit . et si forte aliter et melius concedere
scivit . et dare potuit utpote celestis . terreno .
permanens in eternum : ad eterna transituro. Ab-
stulit autem umbratile regnum cui verum servavit
et eternum ne foret illud transeunti ad istud vel
leve impedimentum. Ne vero cogitaciones hominum timide quorum et incerte sunt providencie
ob impendentis molem discriminis cogitarent pium
Dominum adversus devotum famulum cogitaciones
tantum cogitasse afflictionis . et non eciam pacis:
immanitatem futuri scandali prevenire decrevit im-
mensitatem premissi miraculi . utque tandem hiis[1]
finem imponamus talibus clemencie sue indiciis .
dominus dominancium et instantis glorie . et ex-
tantis gratie sue[2] manifestacionem . preferre servo
suo dignatus est et conferre. Hiis denique beneficiis
et in persecucionis nubilo et in abjectionis luto .
margaritam suo inferendam diademati illustrem exhibuit et ostendit . summa potestas . infinita pietas
inaccessa sublimitas . sapiencie . clemencie[3] . et
magnificencie omnipotentis Dei Patris et Filii et
Spiritus Sancti solius et unius regis seculorum eterni.
Quod vero de quercu opponunt alii viderint ipsi
qui silvestres . et feras et arbores colunt . qui ligna
insensibilia . et bruta animalia hominibus nature sue
consortibus ad ymaginem Dei factis et quod hiis

[1] H.; piis, G. [2] Indiciis . . . gratie sue. [3] H.; gratiæ, G.

amplius eft Dei morte redemptis: preferre nec metuunt nec erubefcunt. Viderint ne forte jurare cogentis et fecuture illius pofteritatis pocius quam juramentum exhibentis prefignaverit aufpicia: arbor ipfa. Viderint et dijudicent utrum eis congruat per quos fanctitatis pariter et libertatis viror et vigor emarcuit et evanuit antique in Anglia ecclefie quod ubi regni fui primordia pulfare ceperunt lignum viride et frondofum fubito exaruit. decorem repente exuit[1]. et confufibilem tenuit nuditatem. In hunc modum fecundum ea que accidiffe dicuntur pro rege noftro beato Haroldo vel contra ipfum aliis fic aliis vero fic fencientibus, nos que parcium fuerunt tetigiffe fufficiat diffinitivum calculum lectoris feu potius cuncta fcientis Dei: examini concedentes. Quantum vero noftrarum intererat virium per hec que non fuperflue ut eftimamus commemorata funt lapides fcandalorum de via tollere. et planum iter facere dictante ut confidimus ipfa rerum veritate[2] conati fumus. Supereft jam ut redeunti et de via longiffima venienti ad nos regi noftro et patrono celeriter occurramus et repatrianti in Anglorum primum. deinde in Angelorum patriam devoto fidelis ftili minifterio pro viribus obfe- f. 17. quamur. Ipfe vero non modo humanum fet et divinum jam accufando et judicando fe. fic ftuduit judicium prevenire ut fit ei pro minimo ab hiis judicari. qui in partem utramlibet odio propenfiores aut favore: juxta humanum diem judicant. crebrius erronie rarius vere.

[1] exuut, H.; exuit, G.     [2] H.; verum reritate, G.

*Quod multis in peregrinatione annis exactis ad Angliam ob exercitandam pacienciam et benignitatem Haroldus rediens Christianum se vocitari fecerit decenniumque in rupe quadam expleverit*[1] *solitarie vivens ; et in hujus temporis Antichristos compendiosa inveccio* . . . . . . *xiij.*

XACTIS igitur in sancto religiose peregrinacionis sudore quampluribus annis alium conversacionis modum corpori jam laboris diuturnitate etateque confecto de cetero censuit imponendum. Didicerat quidem innumeras sanctorum quos adierat virtutes et vitas sanctissimas . decrevitque jam gressum figere . circuitionibus finem dare valefacere ex integro Marthe . cum Maria sedere. Meditacionibus eorum que visu vel auditu perceperat ex dictis bonorum et gestis animum spiritualiter ruminando quo liberius saginare[2] quatinus cum psalmista re et veritate cantare potuisset . *Sicut*[3] *adipe et pinguedine repleatur a*[*nima*] *m*[*ea*] *et la*[*biis*] *ex*[*ultantibus*] *lau*[*dat*] *os meum.*[4] Gustaverat ac tenuit et ipse tum in se tum et in dulci ac

[1] H.M. ; explevit, G.  [2] H.M. ; saginaret, G.
[3] Psalm lxii. 6.  [4] H.M. ; maum, G.

suavi justorum sanctitate . quam dulcis et suavis est sanctorum Sanctus ; factuque ducit optimum in reliquum vacare plenius . ut videat perfeccius . sciat felicius quia Dominus ipse est Deus. Verum ne corporalis vacacio ut est familiare incautis animo inferret feriato ignaviam aut torporem . in illa potissimum vacare terra et quiescere preelegit ex cujus incolatu patiencie et benignitatis majus exercitium majusque argumentum: habiturum se exhibiturumque previdit. Sciebat perfeccionis culmen cujus pectore jam dilatato gerebat amplitudinem . in eo quam maxime eminere quod filius unigenitus summi patris fratribus adoptivis indicere dignatus est et docere . *Orate*[1] . inquiens . *pro calumniantibus et persequentibus vos . benefacite hiis qui oderunt vos . ut sitis filii patris vestri qui in celis est qui facit solem suum oriri super bonos et malos . et pluit super justos et injustos.* Aspirans igitur precordiali affectu ad vere hujus perfeccionis meritum et premium ad quam pocius tendere vel in qua manere terra quam ad illam et in illa debuisset que tot sui persecutores: quot illius possessores . quot in illa potentes tot se odientes . tot ferme se calumpniantes quot sibi vel de se loquentes continet. Nec vero temere jam: tam forti se credit certamini committit discrimini. Non enim ignorat interni sui robur inhabitatoris quem inhabitabat . et a quo inhabitabatur nec vetabatur[2] cum apostolo dicere: *An*[3] *experimentum queritis ejus qui in me loquitur Christus?*

---

[1] Matt. v. 44, 45.   [2] H.M.; verebatur, G.
[3] 2 Cor. xiii. 3.

Tanti hofpitis confciencia fisus Chriftianum fe voluit nominari . ut ei unione jam fpiritus conjunctus[1] communione uniretur etiam vocabuli: quem fe inhabitantem in fe loqui: in fe noverat et operari in fe et pati. Nam et illud corde fibi . opere vero etiam nobis cum Paulo loquebatur : *Omnia*[2] *poffum in eo qui me confortat.* Non fic impii . non fic quos hoftis verfipellis hoftis dejiciens et dejectus . fic armat ut perimat fic roborat ut enervet. Docet enim vos ponere carnem brachium veftrum ut recedat a Deo cor veftrum ut fitis ficut myrice florentes et fteriles . habitetifque nunc in terra falfuginis que fuis fructum cultoribus non producit poft in terra inhabitabili : que fuis incolis requiem non concedit. In hac enim terra : folum fempiternus horror inhabitat. Quis enim habitabit cum igne devorante aut quis habitabit cum ardoribus fempiternis? Quibus tamen[3] poftremis verbis propheticis abfque abufione abutimur . ignium non nefcientes diverfitatem . quorum ifte peccatores fine confumpcione confumit . ille peccata confumendo . peccatores juftificans illuminat pariter et accendit. Quid autem nobis eft de hiis qui foris funt loqui vel judicare . qui ecclefiam immo ecclefias exterius quidem rapiunt et diripiunt . fet intus nec intrant nec inhabitant vineam quidem Domini Saboth[4] . pro poffe fuo vindemiantes et fuccidentes . fet ab ejus cultore jam ipfi precifi . et nifi refipifcant . in ignem eternum in puncto mittendi? Verum[5] quia

---

[1] H.M.; cunjunctus, G.  [2] Philip. iv. 13.
[3] H.M.; tame, G.  [4] H.; Sabaoth, M.G.
[5] H.; Utrum, M.G.

Antichristi facti sunt isti ad[1] nostrum pocius redeuntes Christianum hos sibi relinquamus et suo igni. Nam et nunc teste propheta ignis adversarios devorat . et juxta vitis vere sentenciam : palmes post mittendus[2] in ignem jam ardet. Christianus vero noster novus et vetus . novus : nomine vetus professione[3] . Christo se inhabitante securus jam mundi victor et illius qui in mundo est principis debellator novo marte nova preliandi arte suos aggreditur vincere victores. Contulerat ei suus rex cui spe recuperandi regni amissi jam diu militaverat . ignem caritatis . quo flatu Sancti Spiritus estuante . victricium sibi armorum copiam tribulacionum mallei super incudem paciencie fabricaverant. Hiis pro amisso quidem regno set celesti non terreno . certare didicerat invictissime sciens quia sicut nullo fine ita nec ullo hoste cum illud obtinuisset posset amittere. Appulsus igitur demum in regnum quondam suum periculose quidem habitum set fructuose amissum . armis quibus erat munitus pro regno incomparabiliter meliore viriliter pugnaturus . castrum ingreditur suis copiis satis aptum. In quadam namque rupe secus Dovram sese recipiens . collegit primum se in se ; deinde conscendens a se super se cernebat terram a longe cujus interdum regem quoque oculi sui videbant in suo decore in qua[4] et cum quo etiam ipse certa spe presumebat regnare. Hic juxta decalogi summam decennium in vite solitarie tyrocinio miles jam emeritus complens . vitalia legis divine pre-

r. 18.

[1] H. ; isti ? Ad, M.G.   [2] H. ; postmittendus, M.G.
[3] H.M. ; prefessione, G.   [4] H. ; quo, M.G.

cepta divinius ipfe vivendo certabat pocius excedere quam implere. Noverat enim id quidem virtutis. hoc effe fanctitatis. inchoacionis illud: iftud perfeccionis. Illud quoque neceffarium hoc cenfebat gloriofum. Hic denique confilium illic imperium attendebat. hominum pariter falutem et gloriam: zelantis et procurantis Dei. Non vero multum a loco ubi regnum terrenum pene moriendo pridem ipfe amiferat. Hic locus aberat ubi vitam fic inftituendo degebat. regnoque celorum vim faciendo illud rapiebat. Hic ergo paciencia hic et clemencia viri vires fuas exercebant et perdebant. ubi et preteritus fuus fuorumque lapfus. prefenfque hoftium faftus. memorie necnon. et afpectui fuo quo frequencius ingerebatur. eo benignius ad retribuenda retribuentibus fibi non mala fet pie interceffionis ampla beneficia incitabatur.

*Quod in confinio Wallensium postmodum Haroldus* f. 18 b. *pluribus in locis tempore multo degens pacienter eorum frequencius tulerit assultus . faciem velans panno et nomen nomine alio ne aliquatenus agnosceretur . et quod tandem ad ejus venerationem conversa est immanitas persecutorum* . . . *xiiij.*

ECOLENS vero quia et Ualensibus licet ob justam ut tunc temporis videbatur gentis sue defensionem extitisset quandoque infestus . cupit jam Christianus perferre cum Paulo . quod egerat quondam Haroldus cum Saulo. Pertendit igitur Cancie valefaciens usque in partes Wallie multoque ibi diversis in locis moratus tempore: manebat cum illis et orabat pro illis quem illi non se jam oppugnantem . sed pro se pugnantem indesinenter impugnabant gratis. Accessurus vero ut premissum est in terram sibi ante cognitam ne quavis occasione a quolibet agnitus . virtutis meritum precio vanitatis dum laus oblata jure in eo laudanda prosequitur venditaret faciem suam et nomen proprium omnibus abscondebat . processurus in publicum: velamen panniculi jugiter vultui pretendebat. Nomen requisitus: Christianum se

dici aiebat. Qui enim nominis appellacione universis cicatricum vero fuarum infpeccione quibufdam innotuerat: vultum fimul[1] et vocabulum occultabat. Timebat namque ne forte his indiciis proderetur. Metuebat fiquidem ne vel a fuis fi qui forte fupereffe potuiffent vel ab alienis quoque fi agnofceretur? plaufibus exciperetur feu priftine dignitatis et moderne humilitatis intuitu . feu etiam domeftice neceffitudinis aut familiaritatis obtentu. Nec enim timendum erat ne talem etatem feu converfacionem agens talem: ab hoftibus fi proderetur hoftiliter tractaretur . et durius quam fe ipfe conftruxerat[2]: per ipfos arctaretur. Non erat incertum tamen quia fi eorum notitie exponeretur moleftius utique quam eculeis[3] et carceribus laudibus ipforum et preconiis premeretur. Quis enim tam humilem et mitem . tam benignum et leuem[4] tam mundi rebus inanem . mundique amatoribus fponte defpicabilem videns . prefertim fi quante olim excellencie quanteque affluencie nec non et potencie fuiffet minime lateret . quicquid poffet venerationis et honoris non ei devotiffime exhiberet? De ejus namque parfimonia et paciencia illud in eo mirabile commendatur quod non tam ad injurias pacienciam quam benificenciam rependebat et cariosum jam corpusculum refocillabat pocius quam reficiebat tenuiffimis alimentis. De quo et hoc a quodam religiofo admodum Chrifti fervo accepimus . quia fi quando vel exilem pifci-

f. 19.

[1] H.M.; fimal, G.  [2] H.M.; conftrixerat, G.
[3] H.M.; aculeis, G.  [4] H.; lenem, M.G.

culum edebat . nunquam infumpto[1] uno latere latus reliquum attingebat . aut regirabat . fed vel miniftro vel egeno fi affuiffet : intactum porrigebat. Ejus nimirum vir fanctus intencione rigidiffima complexus exemplum cujus fibi nominis vendicarat participium : maluit temporaliter cum Chrifto . et pro Chrifto jam a Chrifto dictus Chriftianus defpici et affligi: quam mundi favoribus et oblectamentis demulceri . unde et feipfum fevicie Wallenfium ultro duxerat exponendum ponens fibi ante mentis oculos pafchalem Agnum qui fponte feipfum optulit[2] impiis facerdotibus pro nobis immolandum.

Sicut enim[3] Chriftus ambulavit Chriftianus cupiens ambulare Agnum quem forte fequi non poterat per illibatam carnis mundiciam fequi feftinabat quocumque iret tum per mundi cordis puritatem . tum per afflicti corporis paffionem. Paciendi namque fervens amore quafi parum reputans quicquid ipfe fibi carnifex afperitatis intuliffet corpori et inedie effere gentis libenter adivit contubernium . a qua etfi quominus crucifigendum variis tamen modis fe noverat affligendum. Nec fecus quam fperabat et optabat: ab infidis ferinifque homunculis pertulit . verberibus namque feviffimis a latrunculis eorum fepius vehementer attritus quibus etiam poffent dampnis[2] afficiebatur.

[1] H.M. ; confumpto, G.    [2] H.M. ; obtulit, G.
[3] The ufe of the ancient diacritical mark of abbreviation for this word (.n.) goes far to fhew that the fcribe of this MS. was here copying from an original document, quite as old, in point of date, as the actual facts which it propofes to narrate.
[4] H.M.; damnis, G.

Fraudabant eum viatico . vefte fpolibant utque peccunias¹ quas non habebat exhiberet nimiis et exquifitis eum cruciatibus et injuriis contorquebant . faciebant talia homines beftiales . quibus apte fatis congruit quod de Longobardis fanctus Gregorius ait ; " Quorum," inquid,² " funt zinzungie³ pene et gratie fpate." Perferebat vero homo Dei univerfa mente placita⁴ . hylari vultu . ore dulciloquo . manu munifica ; nec quievit pietas hujufcemodi cum impietate conflictus . quoufque illius malum in hujus bono devictum . verecundiam victe imprimeret . victrici gratiam cumularet et gloriam. Pafcebat etenim ac potabat ut vox monet apoftolica inimicos . mulcebat predones beneficiis . mitigabat tortores : miraculo inaudite lenitatis. Congerebat perinde de camino multe caritatis carbones ignis fuper capita eorum . unde mol[l]ita eorum duricia medullitus demum liquefacta colere cepit . et honorare quem folebat illudere et flagellare. Infiftit manus obfequiis . que feviebat plagis. Ingeminat laudes affueta lingua contumeliis. Virtus enim inexperte bonitatis more aromatum quo durius tractabatur forcius redolebat . laciufque diffufa : multis per girum odor vite in

[1] H.M.; pecunias, G.     [2] H.M.; inquit, G.
[3] H.M.; fuzugiæ, G. The reference is to S. Gregorii Magni Epiftolarum, lib. i. xxxi. (Migne, vol. lxxvii, fol. 484.) "quia ficut peccata mea increbantur, non Romanorum, fed Langobardorum epifcopus factus fum, quorum fynthiciæ fpathæ funt, et gratia pœna." The annotator writes, " Synthiciæ funt pacta, conventiones, a Græco συνθήκη. Spatha, gladius ; unde fpatharius ; ... Senfus igitur eft ; Langobardorum pacta, contractus, id eft, jura omnia quæ apud Romanos conftant ex pactis et contractibus, verfantur in vi et ferro."
[4] H.M.; placida, G.

vitam fiebat. Pellebat namque et fugabat fpiramen diabolicum nebulofi furoris: a precordiis brutorum licet hominum illapfa fenfibus eorum fragrancia fuavis fancte illius opinionis. Putares jam plerofque ex hiis: illud ei de canticis affectibus pocius quam vocibus concrepare . *In*[1] *odore unguentorum tuorum currimus anime fiquidem noftre dilexerunt te.*

[1] "Oleum affufum nomen tuum; ideo adolefcentulæ dilexerunt te. Trahe me : poft te curremus in odorem unguentorum tuorum."—*Cant. Cantt.*, i. 1, 2.

*Quod vir Domini Haroldus fugit obsequios quos adierat et diu sustinuerat persequentes et quod voce de celo lapsa designatus sit ei locus pausacionis sue . et quod semiplenis verborum indiciis . sciscitantibus innuerit se fuisse Haroldum et quod scripto successoris sui plenius ostendetur inferius: hujus rei certitudo . . . . . . . xv.*

T vir Domini humilitatis profunde cultor amator quietis custos sollicitus utriusque . ne alterutrius boni saltem exiguum admitteret detrimentum: quos persecuturos censuerat expetendos . inclinatos jam ad obsequia decernit fugiendos. Cedebat in eo jam corporei roboris virtus laboribus quidem cedere nescia . sed annis infracta. Crederes olim roborari pocius quam infirmari genua ejus a jejunio . clunes et pedes meando agilitatem sumere fatigacionem vix sentire. At jam decrepito experiri erat: quia

"Omnia [1] fert etas."

Fusa igitur supplici oracione ad Dominum: locum previderi divinitus sibique jamjam deficienti jam pre sue solius suavissime desiderio

[1] Stat. *Theb.*, iii. 562.

visionis precordiali spiritu languenti solita postulat benignitate concedi: in quo vite reliquum sub silentio optate quietis transfigeret . et felici demum excessu terminaret. Senciens autem per spiritum benignum Dominum pauperis sui pium exaudisse desiderium imponi se fecit vili ju- f. 20. mento . solitoque contentus ministro . iter quo illum Dominus destinare dignaretur aggreditur . pedibus iccirco subvectus alienis: quia virtus jam aberat suis. Recedens igitur scienter nescius . et sapienter indoctus ductu comitatus angelico . Cestrensem demum pervenit ad urbem . Ubi mox die inclinato ad vesperam . mediam ingressus civitatem: cum mansionis locum ministrum inquirere precepisset: vox repente hujuscemodi auribus eorum illabitur . "Vade," inquid,[1] "vir bone ad ecclesiam sancti Johannis paratam ibi accipies mansionem." Attonitus ad audita minister oculo undique circumspectans curioso . edite vocis inquirit prolatorem: sed non comparuit. Nimirum angelum Domini bonum qui itinera sua secum comitatus bene semper disposuisset illum fecisse[2] qui de parata sibi mansione . hec denunciasset viro Dei non fuit incertum. Ipse vero more suo panno ante oculos pendente . et totam pene faciem operiente . aspectum sibi velaverat ne videlicet occurrentibus ob notabilem cicatricum suarum obduccionem stupori esset . vel si agnosceretur eciam veneracioni . vel ne ad mentis abdita . sensibus undecunque occurrenti pateret aditus vanitati. Designant mox digito qui circumstabant ecclesiam

[1] H.M.; inquit, G.    [2] H.M.; fuisse, G.

celesti oraculo sibi designatam: accedit . et gratulanter accipitur . hospes celitus destinatus. Migraverat sane ab hac luce de recenti venerabilis anachorita ejusdem loci casulam suam divinitus proviso cedens sanctissimo successori. Suscepit vero letabunda et gaudens . licet quisnam esset . cercius non agnoscens regem suum filia Syon ecclesia videlicet memorata sedentem ignobile quidem subjugale . sanctum tamen et sibi venientem in omnibus salutarem. Ibidem quoque manens a visitantibus se . et que edificacionis erant ab eo reportantibus . frequenter requisitus an bello ubi rex Haroldus occubuisse ferebatur interfuisset: respondebat . "Interfui plane." Suspicantibus vero nonnullis ne forte ipse esset Haroldus: et curiosius quoat[1] licuit inde sciscitantibus aliquociens[2] ita de se loquebatur . "Quando apud Hastingas dimicatum est: nullus Haroldo me carior habebatur." Hujusmodi ut ita dicatur semiverbiis ancipitem de se nulli opinionem firmabat pocius in suis conjecturis quam in veritatis certitudine[3] confirmabat. Quemadmodum vero rei hujus evidencia universis demum palam innotuerit non nostri sed viri venerabilis quem in ejusdem anachoreseos inhabitacione habuit successorem . verbis inferius exprimetur.

[1] H.M.; quoad, G.    [2] H.M.; aliquoties, G.
[3] H.; certitudinem, M.G.

*Monetur lector ne spernat leccionem quam sentit a nonnullorum opinionibus discrepare . et de triplici occasione contraria existimancium super materia presenti et de Willelmi Meldunensis circa Haroldi fata errore triformi* . . . . . *xvj.*

NTERIM vero lectori nostro humiliter suggerendum existimo ne ista utēque[1] a nostra[2] pravitate digesta ducat spernenda . quia aliter atque aliter plerosque forsan meminit de hac ipsa . et dixisse et scripsisse materia. Manifestum enim est quia non solum plebei relatores immo et illustrissimi rethores[3] non modo diversa sed penitus contraria senserunt . et scripserunt super hiis que facta seu fata Haroldi contingunt. Convincitur autem tum evidenti racione tum et auctoritate non posse esse verum altrinsecus: quod dissonat. Hoc ipsa quidem veritate dictante: sanctus dixit Ieronymus.[4] In sentenciarum vero quas hic ventilamus racione triplex poterit a bene considerantibus assignari contrarietatis seu quod eciam inficiari nullus debet falsitatis occasio. In primis equidem perspicuum

[1] H.M.; utique, G.  [2] H.M.; nosta parvitate, G.
[3] H.M.; rhetores, G.  [4] H.M.; Hieronymus, G.

est quia in multis rei veritas univerfos pene diucius latuit. Hinc odium perfone . feu favor benevolis: commentandi bona malevolis: fimiliter mala de incertis configendi : liberam videbatur ceffiffe facultatem. Hiis facundiffimus aftipulatur in cronicis fuis Meldunenfis Willelmus[1] promittitque fe medium inter obtrectancium . necnon et commendancium partes inceffurum. Crediderim proculdubio ipfum pro viribus veris inftitiffe nec juftis preconiis . nec vituperiis . debitis negociorum merita ultro defraudaffe. Verum quia audita non eciam vifa fcribebat hyftoriarum lege auctoris veritas tuta eft ubi veritas quoque ipfa geftorum : naufragatur. Alias : nec ipfi beatiffimi Evangeliorum fcriptores periculum falfitatis effugerant. Sic Salvatoris pater dicitur Jofeph . fic difcipulorum quidam fratres ejus peculiarius ceteris nominantur . non quod verus fed quod putativus eos pater filios habuerit non quidem naturales fed pocius adoptivos.

f. 21. Secutus igitur opinionem et vero minus affuetus et ifte quod vero jam patet fuiffe oppofitum : hiftorie fue quamlibet veritati pro viribus innixe agnofcitur indidiffe. Ceterum in aliis que de meritis Haroldi vel moribus prout animus tulit aut fama fuggeffit aureo nunc vero piceo commentatus eft ftilo venalius forte exorbitaverit a tramite veri in ipfum vero Chriftum Domini trunculencius deliquit. Tres enim lanceas in ipfum violentus intorfit . quibus non tam illius perfonam quam ipfam contigit

---

[1] The hiftorian William of Malmefbury. The paffages alluded to are in his *Gefta Regum*, ed. Hardy, Englifh Hiftorical Society, 2 vols., 8vo, pp. 339, 383-385, 408-420.

impeti veritatem. Dixit eum ictu fagitte: capite vulnerato oppetiffe[1]. dixit militem qui regi mortuo femur inciderat ducis cenfura victoris: ab exercitu pulfum.[2] Retulit a matre funus regium oblata pecunia a triumphatore Willelmo poftulatum . fed receptum abfque pecunia: apud Waltham tumulatum.[3] Sic in femur . fic in caput fic in omne hominis corpus lingua licencius debachatur[4] oratoris clanculo fcriptitantis . quam militis armata manus in propatulo dimicantis. Verum tam a fagitta oris iftorum quam et a framea manus illorum liberavit Dominus pauperem et inopem quem et rethoribus[5] et regibus multis probavit in pluribus pociorem.[6] Non quidem de omnibus dico dabit Dominus fimpliciter gradienti intelligere que fcribo . fentire que fencio. Temperancius vero fcripfit hujus

[1] "jactu fagittæ violato cerebro procubuit." (W. Malm., *Gefta Regum*, p. 416) ; "aminus lethali arundine ictus mortem implevit" (*ibid.*)

[2] "Jacentis femur unus militum gladio profcidit ; unde a Willelmo ignominiæ notatus, quod rem ignavam et pudendam feciffet, militia pulfus eft" (*ibid.*)

[3] "Corpus Haroldi matri repetenti fine pretio mifit, licet illa multum per legatos obtuliffet: acceptum itaque apud Waltham fepelivit, quam ipfe ecclefiam, ex proprio conftructam in honore fanctæ Crucis, canonicis impleverat." (W. Malm., *Gefta Regum*, p. 420.) To which Hardy adds in a note : "There feems to have been a fabulous ftory current during the twelfth century that Harold efcaped from the battle of Haftings. Giraldus Cambrenfis afferts that it was believed Harold had fled from the battlefield, pierced with many wounds, and with the lofs of his left eye, and that he ended his days pioufly at Chefter. Both Knighton and Brompton quote this ftory. W. Pictavienfis fays that William refufed the body to his mother, who offered its weight in gold for it, ordering it to be buried on the fea coaft.

[4] H.M.; debacchatur, G.   [5] H.M.; rhetoribus, G.

[6] pocior c̄, H.; pocior eft, M.; potiorem effe, G.

ipfius fcriptoris contemporaneus venerabilis admodum abbas Edelredus[1] fuper hec in vita fancti predeceſſoris ejus regis Eadwardi.[2] Dicit quidem aut occubuiſſe Haroldum in prelio aut penitencie refervatum : non fine vulneribus evafiſſe.

[1] H.M.; Ethelredus, G. This refers to Ailred, Abbot of Rievaulx, whofe work "De Vita et Miraculis Edwardi Confeſſoris" is printed by Twyfden in the *Decem Scriptores*, cols. 369-414. The fpecial chapter "De Victoria Regis Haroldi per beati Regis merita" is given in cols. 404, 405.

[2] H.M.; Edwardi, G.

*Quid accidit Walthammensibus circa patroni sui sepulturam pie sollicitis sed mulieris cujusdam errore delusis . . . . . . . xvij.*

ON mediocriter tamen id domini Willelmi aut attenuat in tali errore offensam: quod apud Waltham gestum longe lateque percrebuit. Revera enim ipsos quoque peculiares ae domesticos regis Walthamenses canonicos infandus hic rumor preoccupaverat. In bello siquidem Hastingensi regem occubuisse ora pene omnium loquebantur. Debite igitur patrono suo liberalissimo devocionis clerici non immemores sepedicti . quandam sagacis animi [f. 21. b.] feminam nomine Editham in partes illas ubi dimicatum fuerat quantocius miserunt quatinus vel extincti membra domini sui ad se deferret in sua reverentissime basilica sepelienda. Videbatur enim[1] ad hoc attemptandum[2] . quo imbecillior et infavorabilior hic sexus qui et ipsis cruentis lictoribus minimum suspectus . plurimum vero miserendus censeretur. Hec autem pre ceteris femina com-

[1] H.M.; enim aptior, G    [2] H.M.; attentandum, G.

modius videbatur ad hoc deftinanda[1] que inter milia[2] mortuorum illius quem inquirebat eo quoque facilius decerneret eoque benivolencius tractaret exuvias. quo eum arctius amaverat et plenius noverat utpote[3] quam thalami ipfius fecretis liberius interfuiffe conftaret. Ad locum vero fedis infaufte cum accederet: percepit a multis id nimirum jactabunde difleminantibus circumquaque Normannis regem Anglorum ignominiofe victum cruce femifracto fuper faciem campi cum interfectis jacere peremptum.

Viderit lector quid verius probet. Alii etenim eos qui feminecem fuftulerant regem. hunc quoque rumorem fparfiffe exiftimabant in populo. fuo pariter et illius periculo in hoc profpicientes. quibus indubitato foret exicio. fi illum vivere: hoftis audiret. Inter hec mulieris errorem non mirandum. que defecti. cruentati. jam denigrati. jam fetentis corporis fpeciem minus difcernere valens: pro eftimacione publica truncatum cadaver cum aliud non inveniret quod cercius agnofceret regis proprium: rapuit et fecum attulit alienum. Quod a canonicis reverenter exceptum: indifcufla rei veritate honefte in ecclefia Sancte Crucis fepulture eft traditum.

[1] H.M.; deftituanda, G.   [2] H.M.; millia, G.
[3] H.M.; utque, G.

*Quid frater Haroldi Gurta nomine abbati Waltero vel aliis refponderit fuper fratris fui requifitus cineribus vel fepultura . . xviij.*

N diebus vero regis Henrici fecundi vifus eft tam ab ipfo rege quam a magnatibus terre . et populo Gurta frater Haroldi quem in libro fuo jam dictus hyftoriographus tempore adventus Normannorum aliquid plus puero etatis habuiffe refert prudentia vero animi . et probitate nil diftare a viro. Erat autem jam tunc grandevus valde . et ficut ea tempeftate a multis accepimus qui eum viderant venuftus afpectu . facie decorus . proceritate corporis admodum longus. Hunc vidit etiam pie recordacionis canonicorum regularium apud Waltham abbas primus . dompnus[1] Walterus[2] . a

[1] H.M.; dominus, G.
[2] Waltham, according to Dugdale, *Mon. Angl.*, vi. 57, continued to be a college for about 115 years, according to Harold's foundation, from 1062 to 1177, when Henry I., determined to inftitute Regular Canons in room of Seculars, "quia clerici feculares, qui ibidem huc ufque manferant, mundanis operibus et illecebris illicitis magis quam divino fervitio intendebant." Guido or Wido Ruffus the Dean, being fufpended, refigned in 1174, and in 1177 on the eve of Pentecoft, Walter de Gaunt,

quo una cum fratribus fibi adherentibus in curia regis apud Wodeftocam[1] diligenter fcifcitari ftuduit utrum revera cineres germani fui in fuo ut credebatur monafterio fervarentur. Quibus[2] ille anglice refpondit . "Rufticum" ait "quemlibet habere poteftis . Haroldum non habetis." Ad locum tamen per feipfum venit crucem fanctam adoraturus . Oftenfoque fibi farcofago[3] fratris ut dicebatur: oblique illud intuitus "non" ait "homo fcit " . fic enim jurabat "non hic jacet Haroldus." Vivat in longum et vigeat in Chrifto dominus Michael canonicus probate religionis . camerarius ecclefie Walthamenfis qui multis aftantibus quorum nonnulli adhuc fuperfunt hec ab hore[4] viri fe audiviffe conftanter affeverat. Hiis autem pro legencium commonicione ne perturbet eos varietas incerta fcriptorum breviter nec inutiliter ut confidimus prelibatis . jam ut promiffimus[5] viri fuperius memorati verba ponenda funt quibus manifefte docetur . qualiter fervi fui noticiam Chrifti benignitas plurimis evidentiffime patefaceret indiciis.

---

a canon of Ofeney, was conftituted firft abbot. He died on the eve of Afcenfion Day, 1201. The mention of his name here in the text feems to indicate that his deceafe was recent, and helps to point the MS. to the date which I have affigned to it.

[1] Woodftock, near Oxford.
[2] On the margin of the MS. a monogram of the word *Nota*, to draw the attention of the reader.
[3] H.M.; farbofago, G.    [4] H.; ore, M.G.
[5] H.M.; promiffimus, G.

*Quod viri dei successor de gestis Haroldi beatissimi vera scribens causas gestorum minus congrue bis assignaverit et prime assignacionis discussio et competens prolatis sentenciarum diversarum testimoniis eiusdem improbacio . . . . xix.*

N quibus fidelissimi relatoris id quoque verbis perpendendum est quia sicut res gestas luculenter digessit et vere ita gestorum causas minus ut plerisque videri potest convenienter et provide quod pace tanti viri dictum sit exprimere curavit. Ubi illud tercium adverti potest quod contrarietatis occasionem inter scriptores diximus peperisse. Qualitas scilicet mentis seu intelligencia singula queque referencium qui pro sui affeccione animi . viri sancti[1] affectum propositumque in hiis que gessit mecientes: quid quare fecerit nisi sunt assignatis racionibus intimare. Quorum sensa scribencium credulitas incaucius exprimendo facta plerumque insignia . interpretacione non vera fuscavit. Quod non semel sed secundo bono huic viro in sue

---

[1] H.; sanctissimi, M.G.

narracionis ferie illis videtur accidiffe . qui rationi perfpicue nec non aliorum opinioni amplius innitentes eorum videlicet qui fervo domini familiarius adheferant ipfius quodam modo intimam mentis ymaginem cordibus fuis alcius impreffere. Que vero illa fint quibus minus adquiefcit ipfius ut creditur tenor veritatis opere precium eft breviter difcutere . quo fimplicioribus pro poffe auditoribus vim difcrecionis aperientes . omnem dubietatis caliginem de medio auferamus. Dicit igitur memoratus vir de fancto tunc peregrinante ita. Poftmodum quia natalis foli femper dulcis effe folet inhabitacio: ad Angliam cujus antea rex extiterat concito properavit. Cum autem fapientum diffinicione tritum fit: quia infirmus eft adhuc cui patria fua dulcis eft . fortis vero jam . cum omne folum patria eft . perfectus quoque cui omne folum exilium eft . cui non pateat abfurde dici virum ut ipfe dicit fenectute aridum . diuturnitate itineris utique religiofi confractum . natalis foli ut repatriaret dulcedine attractum? Dicente infuper Domino ad Abraham: *Ingredere*[1] *de tera*[2] *tua* . itemque in pfalmo . *Oblivifcere*[3] *populum tuum et domum patris tui.* Quem etate minorem animi firmitate . et fanctitate meriti . inferiorem pariter et imbecilliorem . tenere non potuit terre fue . populi fui . domufque paterne dulcedo aut memoria duceret jam vel attraheret in omnibus

---

[1] H.M.; Egredere, G. Gen. xii. 1.
[2] H.; terra, M.G. The MS. originally had the word *dextera* written in error, the *x* being now erafed.
[3] Pfalm. xliv. 11.

hiis quo provecciorem eo proculdubio et perfecciorem. Aut hanc omiſſam olim dulcedinem corde ruminanti non continuo illud evangelicum auribus interioris hominis forcius inthonaret:[1] *Nemo*[2] *mittens manum ſuam ad aratrum . et reſpiciens retro aptus eſt regno Dei?* Nec vero perpendit ſcriptor pius quale tunc fuerit illud ejus natale ſolum qualiter immutatum quam ſibi ſuiſque infeſtum quam omni jam ſui reſpectu . et ſi mollioribus adhuc duceretur affectibus . eſſe poſſet eciam grave ſibi ad videndum.

[1] H.M.; intonaret, G.     [2] Luc. ix. 62.

*Secunde affignacionis infirmacio et fcriptoris ad lectorem deprecacio et de difficultate materiam refarciendi a prifcis fcriptoribus varie laceratam. . . . . . . . xx.*

EC fatis validiore[1] paulo inferius racione fulcitur ubi caufam allegat qua Ceftriam aditurus deferuit Salopeffyram. Refert eum ne tribulacio exterior interioris hominis quietem a moderaminis fui ftatu deiceret locum illum deferuiffe in quo . ficut idem perhibet vehementer . et fepiffime a Wallenfibus dampnis[2] et verberibus afflictus . feptennio[3] quietus in fe: et Domino humiliter gracias agens: vifus eft permanfiffe. Que profecto fentencia alia nichilominus[4] adhibita confideracione deprehenditur effe invalida excepta illorum quoque tradicione qui eum fines Wallenfium ob hanc ipfam racionem inhabitaffe affirmant: quatinus pateretur ab illis quos graviffima olim populacione attriverat quamlibet jufta ut putabatur de caufa:

[1] validi ore, H.; validiore, M.G.  [2] H.M.; damnis, G.
[3] H.; feptennio, M.G.  [4] H.M.; nihilominus, G.

quicquid eum perpeti cuncta fuaviter difponentis Dei clemens difpenfacio permififfet. Si enim declinande infeftacionis illius obtentu fedem mutare decreviffet: feciffet hoc utique cicius nec tociens dampnis[1] et verberibus: affligi expectaffet. Nec enim infcius erat in oris eorum in quorum olim medio . triennali ut fertur expedicione hyemando . nimio ipforum periculo intus et in cute ut dicitur eos noverat. Fuit hec quando adhuc comes tanta eos virtute perdomuit . peneque delevit . quanta omnium fequencium ufque in prefens regum vires nequivere.

Tanti enim roboris fuiffe perhibetur cum fuerit audacia fingularis: ut ficut legimus in bello quoque Normannorum nullus ad eum armatorum accefferit hoftium quin ftatim primo ictu equum et equitem deiceret lethaliter fauciatos.[2] Quam adeo mirabilem . jam mutaverat fortitudinem fperans in domino . pennis affumptis volans . et nufquam in volatu deficiens. Hoc autem folum volatili tam forti jam erat formidini ne favoris fcilicet mundani vifco fuarum aliquatenus pennarum virtus infirmaretur fieretque infirmus et non tam volucrum quas pafcit Deus quam illorum hominum fimilis quos pafcit ventus[3]: fi fibi feptem Sampfonis crines adulacionis novacula raderentur. Id folum ergo fugit quod folum formidavit non fane Wallenfis telum fed peccatoris oleum. Sciebat Wallenfes: ignotos habere fufpicacioni . in religione probatos

---

[1] H.M.; toties damnis, G.
[2] On the margin of the MS. a monogram of the word *Nota*.
[3] Cf. Milton, *Lycidas*, "But fwoln with wind," etc.

veneracioni . ideoque illorum afpernari contubernia . iftorum admirari. Vir autem domini hinc quidem juftus et fortis . illic prudens et temperans: afpernantes fortiter expeciit . ut quod meruiffe fe timuit malum jufte pateretur . admirantes prudenter deferuit . ne temperate mediocritatis bono privaretur. Meminit quia olivam pulchram[1] uberem[2] fructiferam . a facie vocis grandis: fubito juxta prophetam combuffit ignis: quamobrem voluit ambulare cum magnis . neque in mirabilibus fuper fe. Quos ergo diu fuftinuerat fupra dorfum fuum fabricantes: peccatores fubterfugit . caput fibi impugnare feftinantes.

Set jam finem fermo flagitat . liber claudendus eft ut que de Haroldo innotefcere neceffe eft: illorum qui hec plenius agnoverunt ftilus evolvat. Benivolum[3] vero lectorem in fui calce libellus ifte finali claufula femper habeat exoratum . quatinus fui auctoris exceffus piis precibus dignetur expiare fecumque fancti Regis Haroldi opitulante interceffione ad portum falutis eterne ipfum pariter optineat[4] pervenire . Multiloquio etiam in prefenti opufculo fcriptoris eo clemencius indulgeat veniam quod[5] difficilius fuiffe confpicit propofitum[6] materiam tot prius veterum ftudiis auctorum difciffam multipliciter et dilaceratam refarcire quodam modo et innovare ac vetuftam . ut ita dicatur ci[m]bam[7] et conquaffatam inter famofos hyftori-

---

[1] H.M.; pulcram, G.   [2] H.M.; uberem, uberem, G.
[3] H.M.; Benevolum, G.   [4] H.M.; obtineat, G.
[5] H.M.; quo, G.   [6] H.M; propofitam, G.
[7] cibu, altered to cibā, H.; cibum, M.; cymbam, G.

arum scopulos in adversum eciam undique nitentibus tanquam ventis . obtrectancium linguis et litteris . ad destinatam perduxisse stacionem. Sit autem Deo adjutori nostro omnis honor et gloria . qui trinus et unus solus imperat benedictus laudabilis gloriosus et superexaltatus in secula.   Amen.

Narratio inclusi qui sancto successit Haroldo de transitu ipsius sanctissimi regis et de miraculis per eum patratis postquam migravit ad Dominum premissa relacione compendiosa de hiis que gessit ac pertulit ex quo terrenum amisit imperium.

CRIPTUM eſt quoniam *tribulacio*[1] *pacienciam operatur paciencia: probacionem . probacio vero: ſpem.* Ad probacionem paciencie . et ſancte ſpei confirmacionem . permittit quandoque Deus ſuos tribulari in preſenti ut liberet a tribulacione perhenni . unde et virum venerabilem Haroldum regem quondam Anglorum permiſit in tempore tribulari . et ab hoſtibus ſuperari et a regno ſuo eici[2] . ne de victoria prius habita ſuperbiret . et in regnum elevatus proſperitatis occaſione amorem divinum poſtponeret . ſet in paupertate poſitus ſanctius et beacius viveret dum a terrenis occupacionibus animum omnino liberum haberet. Igitur

---

[1] 1 Rom. v. 3, 4.   [2] H.M.; ejici, G.

post regni sui amissionem et plagarum suarum quas a Normannis pertulerat curacionem . tanquam peregrinus ad loca sancta per terras multas tunc[1] arripuit . et diu in tali peregrinacione propter Deum laboravit. Postmodum vero senectute aridus . et diuturnitate itineris confractus fatigato corpori alterius modi religionem indicere studuit. Set quia natalis soli semper dulcis esse solet inhabitacio : ad Angliam cujus ante rex extitit concito properavit . ut ibi pauper et vilis: et habitu humilis: residuum vite sue percurreret: ubi quondam rex dives et sublimis . in vestibus amictus preciosis . floruerat . et tanto apud Deum ejus cresceret meritum . quanto benigniorem gereret animum quod cotidie[2] posset adversarios suos intueri . et in regno quod amiserat prosperari et secundum preceptum Domini pro eis Deum fideliter deprecari. Postquam natalis soli fines attigit eremitice vite solitudinem elegit et ibi in pluribus locis conversatus ab omnibus incognitus usque quo cunctis terrenis extremum valefaceret fideliter Deo ministravit. Non autem animi levitate facta est ab eo locorum mutacio . set querebat ubi quiecius serviret Deo. Habuit autem idem vir nobilis ministrum quondam Moyfen nomine . qui michi qui hec scribo incluso in eodem loco apud Cestriam ubi dominus Haroldus heremita et amicus Dei obiit: per biennium ministravit. Eodem vero Moyse . et viris fidelibus referentibus

f. 24.

[1] H.; iter, M.G. This passage clearly shows that G. copied M., and did not collate his text upon the MS. itself.
[2] H.M.; quotidie, G.

ea que fecuntur multa tamen pretermittens breviter et fideliter narrabo. Pervenit autem tandem vir Domini ad Salopeffyra[1] fcilicet ad territorium quod Cefwrthin[2] nominatur . et ibi per feptennium eodem Moyfe illi miniftrante heremiticam vitam ducens valde inquietabatur a latronibus Wallenfibus . et dampnis et verberibus vehementer et fepiffime affligebatur. Que omnia pacienter fuftinuit . in omnibus gracias Deo humiliter exhibuit. Set tamen poftmodum ne tribulacio exterior interioris hominis quietem[3] a moderaminis fui ftatu deiceret :[4] locum

[1] H.; Salopeffyra[m], M.; Salopeffyram, G.
[2] H.; Cefwrthm, M.G. Michel makes no attempt to feek for this place; Giles contents himfelf with faying, "The fituation of this place has not been identified." There can, however, be no doubt that "*Cefwrthin*" is identical with *Chefwardine*, a parifh in the hundred of North Bradford, in the northern divifion of the county of Salop, four miles foutheaft of Market Drayton. The church is dedicated to St. Swithin. According to Eyton, *Antiquities of Shropfhire*, x. 28, etc., Domefday Book enters the manor of Cifeworde-and-Ceppecanole, now Chipnall, in the Staffordfhire hundred of Pircholle, held immediately of the king by Robert de Stafford. The celebrated Countefs Godiva held it at the time of Harold's hermitage there. The name has been varioufly fpelled Chefewurda, Chefworda, Chefwordyn, Chefworth, Chefew'rthin, Chefeword, and fo forth. It paffed into poffeffion of the great family of Le Strange, but Eyton was unaware of the mention of the place in this MS. John Le Strange granted the advowfon of the church to Haughmond Abbey. There does not appear to be extant any documentary evidence fhowing the exact time when the manor paffed out of the county of Stafford and was accounted to be in Shropfhire, but from the text of this paffage it is clear that this had already taken place before the writing of the MS. Eyton fhows incidentally that it muft have been at fome period between 1189 and 1255; at the latter date it enters as a parcel of Bradford hundred in the roll of that hundred.
[3] quietem, omitted, M.G.   [4] H.M.; dejiceret, G.

illum deseruit . et predicto ministro ejus subsequente . Cestriam profectus est. Ibique in capella sancti Jacobi que sita est super fluvium De appellatum : extra muros civitatis in cimeterio[1] sancti Johannis Baptiste per septennium : scilicet usque ad mortem . heremitice vivens religiosissime conversabatur. Utebatur autem ad nudum tamdiu lorica : quousque tota putrefieret . et omnino consumpta videretur. Scissuras vero ejus . et portiunculas dissolutas ministro suo Moysi imperavit ut in fluvium de secreto proiceret[2] . ne ipsum ea fuisse usum alicui hominum pateret. Castissimus quidem fuit corpore . et continens corde humilis et prudens. Cujus condicionis esset semper occultabat ne forte in nimia ab hominibus veneracione haberetur . unde animus elatus a rectitudinis tramite laberetur . et apud Deum humilitatis ipsius meritum minueretur. Raro quidem capella exiit sed oracioni assidue intendit perficiens quod dominus ait. *Quia oportet*[3] *semper orare et non deficere.* Ante oculos suos semper pannum pendentem habuit . qui totam fere faciem velabat ita quod longiuscule iturus ductoris manu indigebat. Quare autem hoc fecerit . minister ejus ignorabat . sed forte hoc agebat ne vultus defecti cicatricum appareret obduccio . vel ne ad cor ejus pateret aditus secularibus vanitatibus dum oculis liber concederetur egressus vel ne ab aliquibus qui eum prius viderant veraciter agnosceretur et ab hominibus veneraretur.

[1] H.M.; cæmeterio, G.     [2] H.M.; projiceret, G.
[3] Luc. xviii. 1.

## De exitu extremo Haroldi.

PPROPINQUANTE autem die exitus venerabilis[1] viri Haroldi perventum est ad hoc quod extreme neceſſitatis urgente articulo vir ſanctus viatici ſalutaris indigeret ſolacio . Unde accedens ſacerdos . quem ego bene novi Andreas nomine . de eccleſia ſancti Johannis . infirmum viſitabat et illi quiquid[2] mos exigit Chriſtianus devote exhibebat. Extremam vero ipſius audiens confeſſionem eum interrogavit cujus condicionis vir fuerit. Cui ille . "Si michi dixeris in verbo Domini quod me vivente quod tibi dixero nulli propalabis[3] ſatisfaciam rationi tue interrogationis." Cui ſacerdos. "In periculo anime mee dico tibi quod quicquid mihi dixeris omnibus erit incognitum . uſque quo extremum efflaveris halitum." Tum ille . "Verum eſt quod rex fui quondam Anglie Haroldus nomine . nunc autem pauper et jacens in cinere . et ut celarem nomen meum appellari me feci nomine Chriſtianum."

[1] H.M.; venerabiliis, G.    [2] H.; quicquid, M.G.
[3] H.G.; propalatis, M.

Non diu poſt hec emiſit ſpiritum : et jam omnium hoſtium ſuorum victor migravit ad dominum. Sacerdos vero ſtatim omnibus nunciavit . quod ei vir Dei in extrema confeſſione intimavit et ipſum eſſe certiſſime re . . . .[1]

[1] Here the MS. ends abruptly at the foot of the page—re[gem Haroldum] . . . M.

*TRANSLATION.*

## THE
# LIFE OF KING HAROLD.

Prologue to the Life of the Venerable Hero Harold, formerly King of the English.

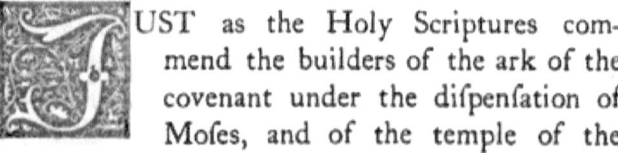UST as the Holy Scriptures commend the builders of the ark of the covenant under the difpenfation of Mofes, and of the temple of the Lord under that of Solomon, fo alfo do they deem thofe men worthy of praife who have faithfully laboured with earneft devotion to offer or prepare things which are neceffary for the building. According to Nehemiah, thofe who derided the builders are overthrown with a terrible imprecation; the rebuilders of Jerufalem, having been rewarded with hereditary titles by Ezra, fanctified an everlafting remembrance of their name and their work to their pofterity. Such a confideration, I truly confefs, vehemently ftimulated my infignificance, although it is of flender value and of tottering ftrength, to contribute fome kind of affiftance to the holy work in which ye toil, reverend fathers. There is added to this ftimula-

tion, moreover, as the turn runs already beyond meafure, on the one fide a brotherly requeſt with friendly perfuafion, on the other fide an anxious admonifhing with a paternal command. I feel, indeed, that it is a work full of labour, yet I truſt it is replenifhed with its own reward, and that it is the performing of your wifhes and the outcome of our own eagernefs. But the pains of a little fpace of time are rightly to be undergone and accepted, with the height of our ſtrength, when in return we are rewarded, not by the applaufe of a frail and fleeting age, but rather by that of a praife and glory which will endure in that place where an eternal honour and fplendour is obtained. Neverthelefs, although to have looked for the reward of tranfitory praife for one's labour on one's work, is to have loſt one's trouble and one's tafk, in the fame way to accept the attraction of a favour, not indeed fought for, although freely beſtowed, is to have deprived one's felf of the reward of internal felf-confcioufnefs and of the praife of the eternal Judge. For we muſt bear in mind how applicable to fuch a pofition is that declaration couched in thefe words: Amen, I fay unto you, they have received their reward.

Your fatherly authority, then, orders, and your brotherly love begs, me to take every watchful care, with affiſtance gathered together on all fides, to promote a remarkable work which, begun indeed excellently, and worthily carried on, ye do urgently prefs forward to a praifeworthy termination, leſt by chance any ſtore of things needful for the completion of this undertaking fhould be wanting to the dutiful tafk. For ye do truly defire that a work of remarkable character fuch as this is, caft in the form of a fingle book, and compiled from various records written by our fathers, and ftudioufly worked out to the praife, and concerning the praife, of the glorious and God-bearing Crofs, with the memorable deeds of your founder (whofe memory we do cheerfully blefs), fhould be rendered famous, and that a tafk dedicated in this way fhould be completed with fuch a cheer, fo to fpeak. The defire of your holinefs is praifeworthy, without doubt, becaufe it is the refult of your devotion, and becaufe it has a good end in view. For it is, indeed, a mark of no undue devotion of yours, that you earneftly defire, by the medium of a literary compofition, to hand down faithfully to a pofterity which is about to be born, the great deeds of fo great a hero. For, of a truth, ye are held bound, by juft fuch a right, to illuftrate by due praife of his virtues, the merits of your own proper patron and everlafting benefactor, as on the other hand ye might fo be, not unduly, accufed of the crime of ingratitude, if you, his guardians and his nurflings, were by your filence to rob pofterity of any knowledge of the efpecially deferving notices of his praife. It cannot be denied that it is the duty of that excellent prudence of yours, to decree that the praifes of one who was a moft devout worfhipper of the Holy Crofs, muft be founded. For, indeed, whatever commendation is deferved by the merits and virtues of its fervant, really belongs altogether to the glory of that Holy Crofs.

And in all this, who does not know how eager my moderate abilities are, in no idle fpirit to fet to work at profecuting fo good a book with a liberal fpirit, willingly employing whatever my ftrength can propofe—yea, rather whatever God's grace can endow me with? If I eat the bread of idlenefs, which belongs to you, or rather to Harold—yea, much rather to the Holy Crofs of you both—the more I behold your ferene faces looking at me, fo much the more ought I properly to dread a feverer condemnation at your hands, if—which God forbid—it fhould chance that I be found, I will not fay ungrateful, but carelefs, after being endowed with fo many benefits, freely and gracioufly beftowed as they indeed are. I will, therefore, comply to the utmoft of my ability with your wifhes. I will fhow the greateft poffible gratitude for your kindnefs, provided that you on your part keep to your agreement with me. That is, that you diligently fcrutinize the contents of my writings, and having examined them, then and then only approve or correct them; rejecting the unpolifhed and badly expreffed diction, but referving, if you think right, the idea, to be expreffed as it fhould be, in a more elegant ftyle. For under God's guidance, the holy band of which you are members, is not lacking in highly educated fucceffors of Bezeleel, Aholiab, or Hyram, men who knew well how to employ, in fuitable places and fitting ufes, the raw material offered up by a fimple-minded congregation as gifts to the Lord. They knew, too, how with the hand of a mafter, and in accordance with the circumftances of the occafion, to polifh each feparate article as deftly as poffible, to prune off the fuperfluous, to arrange the things wanting in order, to adorn the things that were fhapelefs. But all that my want of fkill can venture to undertake, is to hew out from the mountain-fide, and place upon rafts, a quarry in fome fmall degree prepared for a fabric, and to pilot it down the ftream to more convenient fites, and I fhall feel that I have done this when I have handed down, in obedience to your injunctions, a feries of notices which are calculated to benefit the fimple who will take the trouble to ftudy them, gathered together from ancient books, from current writings, from true accounts of the faithful, be they who they may, and gleaned fo as to form the principal points of intereft in this work. So may the gentle and placid breeze of your prayers waft into the harbour of a favourable fhore the fragile bark of my compofition, rigged as it is with the banner of the Crofs for its fail, and the prayers of its faithfulnefs for its figurehead. Amen.

  End of the Prologue.

HERE BEGIN THE CHAPTERS.

I. WHAT a mirror of cheerfulnefs and gentlenefs fhines forth in the acts of King HAROLD. How he was the brother of the Queen, whom the holy Edward married. How his father Godwin, efcaping the fnare of King Canute, received the latter's fifter to wife; and how Harold fignally triumphed over the vices of thofe who brought him up.

II. How Wales was nearly deftroyed by Harold; and how he recovered from paralyfis by the virtue of the Holy Crofs of Waltham.

III. How Harold built, enriched, adorned, and regulated the Church of the Holy Crofs at Waltham; and how Henry, King of the Englifh, abolifhed the fecular canons, and diftinguifhed the place by the appointment of regular canons.

IV. How it was divinely ordained that this man fhould be raifed to the pofition of King, and, after having defeated his enemies, fhould in his turn be conquered by other enemies and depofed from his kingdom; and concerning a very pious anchorite, who had been a fervant of Harold after he became a hermit himfelf.

V. How a certain Saracen woman found him half dead amongft his affailants, brought him to Winchefter, and healed him as he lay there concealed for two years; and how he fought out the Saxons and Danes to collect allies againft the Normans, but was unfuccefsful.

VI. How at length, coming to himfelf, he perceived that God was oppofing him in his worldly path; wherefore, conforming himfelf to the Crofs of Chrift that he might the better triumph over the old enemy, he rejoices that he has fuffered defeat at the hands of men.

VII. How he entered on a long pilgrimage to obtain the prayers of holy men; and how, before he became a King, he vifited the refting-places of the holy Apoftles.

VIII. The admiration of the writer, with a brief exclamation on the goodnefs of God, by which it happens that the fins even of the elect work in them for good.

IX. How many things are faid by many people about Harold's fin; and concerning the oak hard by Rouen, under which he made the oath, which remains, though ftript of its bark, to this day.

X. The excufe fome make for Harold, whereby, exonerating him from perjury, they affert that it was with the fanction of God and confent of the holy Edward that he became King; and concerning the vision of the Abbot Elsinus, in which the holy Edward declared that Harold should be conqueror over the Norwegians.

XI. A wonderful account concerning a Holy Cross which is alleged to have bowed its head to Harold as he was hastening to battle, and certain other very astounding miracles concerning this Cross, proved to be undoubtedly true.

XII. Different interpretations of different men concerning the above-mentioned signs of the bowing Cross and the withered oak; and how Harold, by judging himself favourably, anticipated the divine judgment and fears not man's.

XIII. How, after many years spent abroad, Harold, returning to England for the purpose of exercising his patience and meekness, caused himself to be called CHRISTIAN, and lived ten years in certain rock in solitude; with a short invective against the Antichrists of that time.

XIV. How Harold afterwards spent a long time in various places on the borders of the Welsh, bore their repeated assaults in patience, hiding his face with a cloth, and changing his name for another left he should by some means be recognised; how at length the cruelty of his persecutors was changed into veneration for him.

XV. How Harold, the man of God, avoided the obsequious who persecuted him, whom he had approached, and long borne with; and how a place of rest was appointed for him by a voice that fell from heaven; and how he hinted in ambiguous words to thofe who afked him that he was Harold; and how the truth of the matter will be fhown more fully in the account given by his fucceffor.

XVI. The reader is advifed not to defpife the reading which he feels differs from the opinions of fome; and concerning the three occafions of thofe who think differently about this prefent fubject; and concerning the threefold miftake of William of Malmefbury on the fate of Harold.

XVII. What happened to the people of Waltham in their holy anxiety concerning the burial of their patron; and how they were mifled by a woman's miftake.

XVIII. How a brother of Harold, Gurth by name, replied to Walter the Abbot, or others, when afked concerning the afhes or the burial of his brother.

XIX. How the fucceffor of the man of God, writing a true account of the deeds of the moft bleffed Harold, has on two occafions affigned inappropriate reafons for his actions; with a difcuffion on the firft reafon, and a full difproval of the fame by the production of the evidence of various opinions.

XX. The weaknefs of the fecond reafon affigned, and the writer's warning to the reader; and on the difficulty of patching up materials torn indifcriminately by ancient writers.

HERE END THE CHAPTERS.

HERE BEGINS THE LIFE OF HAROLD, SERVANT OF GOD, FORMERLY KING OF THE ENGLISH.

*CHAP. I.—What a mirror of cheerfulness and gentleness shines forth in the acts of King Harold. How he was the brother of the Queen, whom the holy Edward married. How his father Godwin, escaping the snare of King Canute, received the latter's sister to wife; and how Harold signally triumphed over the vices of those who brought him up.*

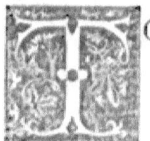O review the actions of the most illustrious and rightfully appointed King HAROLD, at this time duly and lawfully crowned, is nothing else than to display to pious minds a most brilliant reflection of a divine serenity and meekness. And that this may the more clearly appear we will take care to show forth to our readers clearly and briefly the beginning, progress, and ending of his warfare with the world and with Christ. We shall, indeed, have spoken truth when we called him a king most illustrious and lawfully crowned, for by ruling

himself aright and by submitting himself humbly to Him, to serve whom is to be a king, he obtained first a crown of justice, and afterwards a crown of eternal glory. Godwin, a most powerful Earl, begat him from a sister of Canute, King of the English and the Danes, which Harold was brother indeed of the revered Queen whom the King and most holy confessor Edward had married. And although she had been united in an auspicious marriage with him, yet short of consummation, and though both of them, forsooth, preserved their flower of perpetual maidenhood, she was yet a cause of much preferment to her father's family. It is plain, however, that her father, or some of the other members of her family, had been heavily branded with the mark of treason and other crimes.

Godwin, indeed, first entangled himself in these misdeeds, from the necessity of averting an imminent destruction, but afterwards he wanders farther in deceit. Compelled to use deceit under pretence of ensuring his own safety, while once he yields to his wishes, he afterwards committed fraud more freely when he saw his prosperity declining. For when the above-mentioned King of Denmark had usurped the diadem of England, and he saw that Godwin, a man endued with incredible cunning, and no less audacity, was gradually rising to a high position, he himself, a foreigner, began to fear the bold spirit of this young native, armed as it was with power and craft. And although he had found his industry very useful to him on many occasions, yet conceiving in his mind something of the spirit of Saul, he determined to ruin by trickery this most strenuous despoiler and champion, since it was not easy to crush him openly except by spiteful malice. Having thought out, therefore, a plan, he sends Godwin into Denmark, as if on important business concerning both kingdoms, having in his heart some such thought as this: "Let not my hand be upon him, but the hand of the Danes." Now as he was sailing along in mid-ocean, in a vessel fitted with the most lavish appointments, a suspicion began to agitate the mind of the youth. For he was bearer of letters sealed with the King's signet, one for each of the chief men of that country, the contents of which he was quite ignorant. Breaking, therefore, carefully one of the seals, he learnt from the brief enclosure that he would be shortly given over to the punishment of death, when he arrived in port, if he were to discharge any further his duty as letter-carrier. For the tenour of the writing was that whoever should first learn the contents of the letter, was immediately to strike off the head of its bearer, Godwin by name.

This new Uriah grew pale when he found that his destruction was being compassed by the King, and prepares (to make a long story short) to escape the trick by another trick. This is what he did: he broke open and took out each letter from its seal, and substituted a fresh letter written by the clever hand of a clerk, the substance of which was that Godwin was to be received with great and universal rejoicings; to receive in marriage the

King's fister, and that they all were to yield him obedience in what concerned the King's busines, as they would the King himself if he were present. Thus the King's command was changed to the King's advantage. Thus the soldier changes his soldier's pay; thus an undeserved punishment is unaccomplished, and a glory that is deserved accrues to him who earned it; thus at length the King receives as a brother him whom he had hitherto found but a useful soldier, and making him soon after a state officer, found in him for the future an ever-watchful and prudent minister.

Though Godwin was received with much favour by the Danes by this occurrence, yet he came to be on ill terms with many of his own family; and some members also of the royal family he destroyed by treachery, of whom one was the brother of the holy Edward: and thus not only against his fellow-countrymen, but also against his natural lords he committed not a few offences. But on this matter let him who wishes to know seek elsewhere. As far as pertains to the subject in hand, it is enough that we have just briefly touched on such things, left we should seem to have passed over, without consideration, those other matters which we know that people, who understand little about them, have perverted to the discredit of Harold, the servant of God, for wise men see aright that these things pertain in the highest degree to his renown. For he who, by divine favour, has overcome a vice which, as they would have it, nature has inflicted, and which social habits have formed, has certainly gained a greater victory in that he has overcome and got rid of the felf-fame vice in which he was born and reared; for though Harold even, it is afferted, feems to have given way to vice in his youth, he was confidered to have fuffered violence by his nature and rearing. It is plain, then, that, by the help of Him who from the fame lump of clay makes one veffel to honour and another to difhonour, this circumftance, which had been caft up againft him to his difcredit by ignorant men, was turned by Harold to his virtue's benefit, and to the advancement of his honour. Thus a thorn brings forth bright red rofes, and produces, fo to fpeak, fnow-white lilies, from whofe natural functions the meaner property of the thorn fubtracts not, but rather adds to it, from the combination, an increafe of beauty.

CHAP. II.—*How Wales was nearly destroyed by Harold; and how he recovered from paralysis by the virtue of the Holy Cross of Waltham.*

BUT how Harold excelled in strength of body, and how famous he became for shrewdness of mind and vigour in arms, was proved by the way he subdued Wales—aye, and nearly destroyed it to extermination. These victories gave him a conspicuous position even during the lifetime of the holy Edward; and through them he acquired, by his bravery, a peace and tranquillity most serviceable to the King and the whole kingdom.

Meanwhile, though he seemed to be greater than his contemporaries in uprightness and power, and even seemed to outshine the highest princes of the kingdom, the hand of the Almighty, which strikes as well as heals, afflicted his flesh with a grievous stroke, in order that he might obtain by his present and future wounds a remedy for his soul. Physicians call paralysis that species of disease by which a man's body, when affected by it, forgets its proper functions, and deprives him of his accustomed duties, for it suddenly renders the part which it has attacked, or the whole of the body, senseless, torpid, and, as it were, dead. Harold, suddenly attacked and prostrated by this affliction, becomes an occasion of an extraordinary sorrow, for all people grieved for him, especially the King; for the latter, as if by some presentiment of future things, loved Harold, and held him dear beyond all others, though it is said that he looked on some members of that family with a certain degree of suspicion and hatred. And it was not the nearness of kinship, pleasant though it was, nor that excellence of honour and singular industry with which he was endowed, but simply a divine inspiration which, it is thought, produced in this most pious King's mind such a predilection and favour towards Harold. It tends, indeed, to Harold's honour at this period, that a man, full of God, and not ignorant on many occasions of the divine purpose, should love him, and love him the more intensely that he foresaw that Harold should be an everlasting co-heir with him in heaven, rather than his temporary successor on earth. Therefore the King's own special physicians, besides others selected from all quarters by entreaty or payment, gather round the sick man, and try everything that art or conjecture can suggest, but the power of man cannot put aside the hand of the Almighty.

The sad news reached the ears of the King of the Alemanni, who was both near akin to the

King and clofely united to him in affection and friendſhip. At his Court there dwelt a certain phyſician named Ailard, a man moſt trufted by reaſon of his double practice in the art, as well great ſkill as experience, but, what is of greater value, the grace of God ſhowed him much favour in effecting the cure of the ſick. Him therefore the Emperor refolved to fend with all ſpeed to his dear friend the King, that he might apply his cure to the vigorous young man. On being led to the ſick man Ailard carefully examined the nature of the illneſs, and devoted every attention to him; but every labour is of no avail when a heavenly worker operates in oppoſition to the art of man.

At that time a ſtone figure of our crucified King had recently been revealed and difcovered by the heavenly direction, which, having been brought by God's defire to Waltham, was famous in that place for its miraculous virtues. The phyſician therefore, after confideration, perceiving that the Author of Nature was acting in oppoſition to the powers of Nature's art, and that the whole fyſtem of the lower nature was being thoroughly deadened by the counteracting influences of Him who created nature, forthwith concluded that the man was being afflicted by a ſtroke of His power, from whofe hand there is none who can deliver. And foon, as became a truſtworthy and prudent man, he did not delay, as he was unable to cure him by his hand, to procure a remedy by his mouth. For, unlike deceitful and lying doctors, he was willing that the help which he already felt could not be given by him fhould be obtained from other fources. He did not, however, leave the fick man in defpair, but directing him from a hope that was vain to a hope that was well founded, he perfuaded him to put his hope in Him who is the falvation of them who truft faithfully in Him. And that he might the quicker deferve to tafte the joys of a much-defired health, he exhorts him for his profit to attend to the offices of the Crofs which giveth falvation, and to vow a vow to it, as his inward devotion might dictate to him.

The fick man liftened to the plan for his recovery in a fenfible fpirit, and fends with all hafte to the place where the miraculous Crofs difplayed its mighty gifts. He prays with great earneftnefs that the guardians of the place, whofe peculiar duty it was to minifter at the health-giving fymbol, would deign to obtain for him by their hearty prayers pardon for his fins and alleviation of his fufferings; in a word, health for both the inner and outer man. Nor was the mercy of the Saviour long wanting to him who afked for health with a faith unfeigned, for foon the pain and weaknefs of his body grew lefs; but as he became ftronger his love and devotion for the obfervances of the Holy Crofs wonderfully increafed. And thus reftored in a fhort time to perfect health, he proved by acts of magnificence how indebted and devoted he was to the medicine by which he had regained his health. For coming to the Holy Crofs of Waltham, he paid the vows he had made for his health, offered coftly prefents, gave rich gifts to the attendants, commending himfelf to the guardianfhip of that glorious Crofs, and intending to endow it with ftill more exalted honour. Rejoiced, he at length departed from the place in body, but not in fpirit, and prefented himfelf fafe and found to the King, and to the Queen his fifter. The Queen congratulates her brother: the King rejoices with his foldier: the whole Court is glad with a joyous exultation, not becaufe Harold had recovered his health, but becaufe it was from Heaven he had recovered it. All, indeed, with one mind applauded; but the King, as he was holieft, rejoices with greater feeling. He indeed excelled all others in a double joy, becaufe he was wont to find delight in the virtues of Chrift, who brings to pafs fuch holy works, and to feed on thofe advances of devotion and faith which the accomplifhment of fuch miracles was calculated to ftrengthen in the love of the fame moft Holy Redeemer.

*CHAP. III.—How Harold built, enriched, adorned, and regulated the Church of the Holy Cross at Waltham; and how Henry, King of the English, abolished the secular canons, and distinguished the place by the appointment of regular canons.*

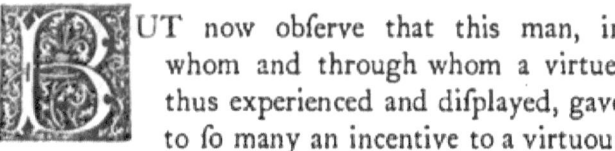UT now observe that this man, in whom and through whom a virtue, thus experienced and displayed, gave to so many an incentive to a virtuous life, could think or speak of nothing else but how he could make an excellent and fitting return for such divine benefits, and how he could, in compensation, give joy to that holy Cross with an honour worthy of a health restored. But in proportion as he applied himself more zealously for the Cross's honour, and strove for its glory, so much the more exceedingly did the favour of Heaven enrich him with increase of virtues and devotion, with which manner of exchange he was greatly delighted, and endeavoured the more intently, by displaying gratitude for gifts he had received, to deserve still more valuable benefits.

He confiders, alfo, that he is bound, for thefe fubftantial favours, to that man whofe heavenly piety had unlocked to him the approaches to fo many privileges, and refolves to prefent him with a reward worthy of his faith and devotion. For there were only two clergy there to pray and take charge of the fervice and worfhip of the Crofs, though they, indeed, feemed content with their fmall emolument and humble dwellings.

But this excellent man, eager to exalt the place and its worfhip with all claffes of its worfhippers, propofes to build there a new temple, to increafe the number of attendants, and to augment their revenues; and in order that its fame and the throng of its clergy might difplay the place in the eyes of mankind, ennobled as it had been by heavenly gifts, more famous and more glorious, he caufed, by a prudent arrangement, fchools to be founded there, under the direction of Mafter Ailard, the preferver of his health, as has been juft now narrated. Nor was he flow to bring forth that which he had conceived in his mind. Foundations of a large church are rapidly laid; the walls rife; lofty columns at equal diftances unite the walls with interlacing arcades or vaults; a roof of leaden plates keeps out the wind and the inclemencies of the weather. The number of clergy is increafed from a fhameful two to the myftic twelve of the company of the Apoftles, and for this excellent reafon, that the fame number of men who had told forth Chrift's glory to the world from the beginning, might ferve in eternal praife in the temple of His holy Crofs.

He also, with a splendid liberality, endowed them with estates and possessions, that they might have sufficient for their necessities; and he obtained a confirmation of these gifts by the King's authority.

Now, if we attempt to describe at length the number of gifts, the value and varied character of the vessels and ornaments with which he ennobled this house of God, the multiplicity of facts might perhaps detract from the exactness of the narrative. But lest the account of his munificence should be lost altogether, or in this particular—and it is known that a violent jealousy has aimed at this— it is worth while to endeavour, with a spirit of fervent zeal (since the real substance of the facts themselves has been lost), to make known to those who wish to consider them, the shadows, so to speak, of the facts. We have therefore thought good to insert on the present page an account of those things which, through jealousy of Harold, as they say, were abstracted from the Church of the Holy Cross by William, the first Norman King of the English, and carried off to Neustria. For that King, as we read, carried off to Normandy, from Waltham, seven shrines, of which three were gold and four silver-gilt, full of relics and precious gems; four books of Holy Writ, ornamented with gold, silver, and gems in their bindings; four large gold and silver censers; six candelabra, of which two were gold and the rest silver; three large pitchers of Greek work, silver and gilt; four crosses worked in gold and silver and precious stones; one cross that was cast from fifty gold marks; five most precious priestly vestments, ornamented with gold and gems; five hoods, ornamented with gold and gems, in one of which were twelve gold marks; two copes, ornamented with gold and gems; five chalices, two gold and the rest silver; four altars with their relics, of which one altar was gold, and the other silver-gilt; one silver wine-horn, valued at one hundred shillings; ten phylacteries, one of which was prepared from two gold marks and precious gems, and the others from gold and silver; two dulcimers; some saddles for women, worked with much gold; and two bells of great value.

These, and very many other things, which it would take a long time to mention, and which the ambition of the Normans would consider incomparable, are known to have been offered to the Holy Cross by Harold in his piety, and taken away by William through hatred. The latter, however, seems to have palliated the heinousness of the robbery by an easy kind of compensation—by disseminating a clear account of the progress of events by which the Cross was discovered and conveyed to Waltham, wherein it is also more fully expressed what, and how many, things the holy man, in a wonderful warmth of devotion, presented to the holy place, either in estates, or various revenues, or in a multitude of things pertaining to the service or adornment of the church. But as my pen is in haste to explain what the worshipper of the Cross did and suffered after he offered himself as a sweet sacrifice to the Lord, bearing his crofs now daily and following Chrift, we proceed to relate what he gave from his own refources, and confecrated to the Crofs as a facrifice of juftice ; which things, indeed, after the removal of many of the moveables, whatever he affigned to the place in lands and vills, or churches and other revenues, to all appearance it ftill poffeffes, without great diminution, yet not, as is faid, without fome lofs. But the conftitution of the Church of Waltham, we fee, was formed afrefh, to a high ftate of perfection, in our time by King Henry the Second, of divine memory. For the canons, who were under a ftrict rule and difcipline, dedicated by Harold to their facred watches, finking through the gradual lapfe of time to fecular purfuits, had put before the facred canonical rule the emptinefs of fecular life. For deriving their name from both words, the "fæculum" and the "canon," they divided the meaning of their name in reverfe order, for lufting after fecular things and defpifing the canon rule, they weighed the knowledge of the latter with the pleafures of the former in a falfe balance; wherefore cafting afide their facred duties, they, who ought to have fpent their time in the halls of the Lord's houfe, ftrutted about in the common paths of the world. Thefe men being at length removed from their office by the holy zeal of the above-mentioned King, the fame place is ennobled by the inftitution of regular canons. They happily, uniting the Latin rule with the Greek canon, preferve in their life the virtues of the double word and the fimple matter, fo that they ought to be objects of the greatest veneration both to the Greeks and the Latins. These men Henry most honourably adorned with offices built for regular canons; but Harold, with the kindest thought, increased their incomes. For by these men the Lord's flock, which served the Lord there in holiness and righteousness, is supported; by them day by day innumerable crowds of travellers obtain all the benefits of humanity; at their hands the traveller and the hungry man receive food and provisions; from them the sick man receives attention, and he who is cold a covering, and the stranger and foreigner a roof to cover him—in a word, everyone who is in need obtains at the hands of these men assistance suitable to his necessities.

*CHAP. IV.—How it was divinely ordained that this man should be raised to the position of King, and, after having defeated his enemies, should in his turn be conquered by other enemies, and deposed from his kingdom; and concerning a very pious anchorite, who had been a servant of Harold, after he became a hermit himself.*

HO knows how the bones of a man are framed in the womb of her who is with child? And who has learnt, or who can learn, what is best for a man in his lifetime? One man generally rules another to his hurt. Sometimes a man is subdued and subjected by one man to another for his good. Thus Chanaan is in bondage to his brother as a servant of servants; thus the hands of Joseph, given over to bondage by his brothers' jealousy, did service in Chophmos; thus, too, our Harold, to return to our subject, is suddenly raised, as it were, on the wind, and is in a moment violently thrown down. He is raised to be King by the acclamation of the kingdom; he returns a victor

from the battle in triumph, having flain the barbarians who had attacked him. He fears not to hear that his late enemy has come upon him, but jeers at him; he runs to attack his deftroyer, as though he would at one blow deftroy him. He joins battle, and falls; he attacks, and is cut down—he is indeed cut down and fallen, but is it to his deftruction or his folly? Will that hand of the crucified King, from which came forth a writhing ferpent, fuftain him? That hand, indeed, permitting it, the enemy's fpear pierced his bones and nearly every limb, and grievoufly wounded him.

All thefe things happened to Harold by the direction and wonderful difpenfation of that fame hand, in order that in the womb of the pregnant Church the bones of a man fore-ordained before fecular times, and deftined by God to be born, and by all thefe means to pleafe God perfectly, might be fafhioned. For conceived through piety according to the inward man, he grew and was increafed towards God in thefe exercifes, and was formed and ftrengthened fo that at length, like Jacob, when Rachel departed on account of pain in parturition, he obtained a Benjamin for a Benoni. For he who to his mother feemed a fon, forfooth, of angelic pain and death, by God his father, who had ordained that by this event a people haughty in mind, rough in ill-doings, and cruel in all kinds of treachery, fhould be fupplanted, he was made by a wonderful transformation the fon of his right hand. But as it was

K

noifed abroad by common converfation how Harold had fucceeded to the earthly kingdom of the moſt bleſſed Edward (himſelf tranſlated to a heavenly kingdom), and how he had triumphed over the Norwegians with Edward's help, and how bravely and with what impulſe and unpreparedneſs, from an exceſſive ſteadfaſtneſs of purpoſe, he went againſt the Normans who were attacking him, and how, with his comrades ſlain, he fell on the enemy ſingle-handed, we, God helping us, will write in our account of thoſe things which happened by the divine agency through him and concerning him, after the faƈts narrated above, which we know have eſcaped the notice of moſt chroniclers.

Some of theſe things we heard from a certain hermit of venerable life, Sebricht by name, who, while he lived, was a ſervant for many years to the holy man; and others from equally truſtworthy authorities, who have related theſe faƈts to us with a certainty which has proved them to be true. And further, thoſe things which happened after his death through power from heaven, and which will be written on this page, have been written by thoſe who were preſent when they happened, and have been handed down to us. But the above-mentioned man of God, once Harold's moſt devoted ſervant and follower, when he departed from this world, and it was clearly ſhown by his miracles that he had gone to heaven, emulated his example in doing good moſt fervently, deſiring to arrive at ſuch a point of holineſs as he had reached, and being zealous to work in as similar a way as he had walked. Therefore, because he knew Harold had done so, he undertakes the toil of a pilgrimage, and becomes a voluntary exile from his native soil, that he might be worthy to become a holy man and a servant of God. With naked feet he leaves the borders of the city of Chester, where he left the treasure which he had preserved there for so many years, taking only a portion for the crown of his heavenly King, but leaving the rest dug up upon the ground; and thus stripped of all worldly desire he goes forth on his pilgrimage.

Thus bare and unencumbered, intending to approach the Lord's Cross on the spot where that Cross was fashioned for the Lord's body, to visit His glorious sepulchre, and to adore the spot where His feet rested, he at length departs from England; and, hoping to bedew with his tears the resting-places of other holy men as Harold had done, to listen to strange languages which he knew not, and to undergo with joy no small tribulation for Christ's sake, he enters the country of strangers. At length, having accomplished his vow, after many wanderings which there is here no space to mention, he returns to his native country as Harold had done. And on his return he betook himself to a town in the Oxford district called Stanton, and, confining himself there, led a severer life till the time of his death than those who are confined and imprisoned for their crimes. Here, becoming an object of veneration and affection to all religious people, he was wont to be fought out and vifited by many for the fake of a mutual edification.

For he had become well known as a man moft devout, felf-contained, affable to all, benevolent to many, well-wifhing to all. By thefe means and in this way there arofe a goodly odour of Chrift, and as all were borne along in the odour of his holy deeds, I alfo, an infignificant perfon, as it were, among greater ones, was carried along with the reft and became clofely bound to him by a chain of love. But I, when ftill of a tender age, and young in the profeffion of religion, had vifited him often through older meffengers, but fometimes in my own perfon, and was at laft admitted to the inmoft fanctities of a familiar friendfhip. At length, when I was older, I advanced fo far that he would fcarcely hide any of his fecrets from me which feemed ufeful for my inftruction as I talked with him on the ftate of the inner man. And he, though he was country-bred, and ignorant of any language but Englifh, he yet held a wonderful and admirable opinion concerning religion, and was clever in expreffing himfelf in his own idiom; as he ufed to fay concerning myfelf: " Let me fay what I think—I believe that the fum-total of my falvation confifts in patience and hope." He would add how many things the Lord had fhown him in the fhape of many and great tribulations, and how mercifully he had, by converting him, given him new life, and how powerfully he had led him from the depths of earth. He would mention, too, what fufferings he had undergone in the body, and in mind, enumerating and diftinguifhing the weaknefs and various affections of both—the wicked affaults of devils, and the no lefs bitter infults of men; and he would add: "In all thefe trials which came upon me, an all but fhipwrecked wretch, my only hope was in the crucified One, my anchor; and leaning firmly on this I faw, after a time, all my troubles, which I had but juft before deemed more intolerable than death itfelf, pafs away, as it were, into foam and afhes. I have indeed borne," faid he, "fuch and fo great afflictions of the flefh (to flee from which I have confined my miferable body like fome untameable beaft in the narrownefs of this prifon) that an ignorant man would fcarcely believe could be fuftained by any body, though it were made of iron or ftone."

Thefe things he ufed to relate, not boafting of himfelf or of his labours for Chrift, but he thought, like fome veteran telling the familiar experiences of his labours, that I, trembling on the brink of the fame untried ftruggles of my fpiritual apprenticefhip might be animated and ftrengthened by their recital. Of fuch things he would fpeak with much feeling, not deploring the hardfhip of his fufferings, but giving forth with a wondrous fweetnefs a memory of that confolation and fpiritual grace which he had found to be the alleviation of his trials.

Thefe matters concerning the man's life and manners we thought it not out of place to infert into thefe pages, in order that from the piety of the pupil it may the more plainly be fhown on what a pinnacle of perfection the life and converfation of the teacher fhines forth. He, indeed, making mention of Harold, would call him his mafter, rejoicing that he had in heaven an advocate whom, when on earth, he had as a preceptor. This, then, is the man by whom, as has been faid above, as well as by others who knew the man of God, and how his pofition of life was ordered and changed according to place and time, thefe things have been arranged and made known. And of thefe fome were ignorant that Harold was once, when he lived, a crowned king, but were witneffes of his converfation and knew well in what places he lived from the time when he fpent his life in folitude in England. For he, dreading from his heart the glory of the world, of which he had experienced fuch ignoble and unhappy refults, when he refolved to live in his own country, took a new name, and changed from time to time the place of his dwelling, left by fome chance it fhould be betrayed to anyone. But we will difcourfe of thefe things in their order below. Let us now from this exceffive digreffion proceed without more delay to the narration of what we have already begun.

CHAP. V.—*How a certain Saracen woman found him half dead amongst his assailants, brought him to Winchester, and healed him as he lay there concealed for two years; and how he sought out the Saxons and Danes to collect allies against the Normans, but was unsuccessful.*

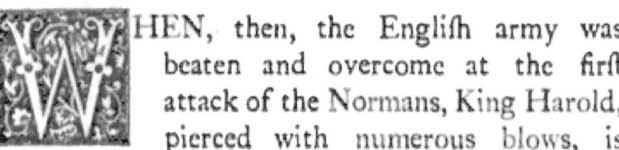HEN, then, the English army was beaten and overcome at the first attack of the Normans, King Harold, pierced with numerous blows, is thrown to the ground amongst the dead; yet his wounds, many and deathly though they were, could not altogether deprive of life him whom the goodness of the Saviour had most happily ordained to restore to life and victory. Thus, as the enemy's host departed from the scene of the slaughter, he, who the day before was so powerful, is found stunned and scarcely breathing by some women whom pity and a desire to bind up the wounds of the maimed had drawn thither. They act the part of Samaritans by him, and binding up his wounds, they carry him to a neighbouring hut.

From thence, as is reported, he is borne by two common men, franklins or hinds, unrecognifed and cunningly hidden, to the city of Winchefter. Here, preferving the fecret of his hiding-place, in a certain cellar, for two years, he was cured by a certain woman, a Saracen, very fkilled in the art of furgery, and with the co-operation of the medicine of the Moft High, was reftored to perfect health. On regaining his ftrength thus, he thought he would prove by great deeds the courage of his royal fpirit which his foul had not loft in the overthrow of his body. Already had the nobles of his kingdom, as well as the people, bowed their necks to the yoke of the conqueror; already had nearly all his chiefs either perifhed or been driven from the country, leaving their anceftral honours to be divided and poffeffed by ftrangers.

Harold, therefore, beholding the deftruction of his own people and the fuccefs of the enemy, groaned in fpirit, and forrowing more for his country's troubles than his own, refolved that he would perifh with his people or procure affiftance for them. He croffed over, therefore, to Germany, the home of his race, with the intention of proceeding to Saxony; but grieves to find that already the miferable overthrow of his nation is common talk in all quarters. He earneftly begs his kinsfolk to lend their affiftance to one of their own ftock; he declares that the misfortune of fo fudden a difafter was not to be attributed to the ftrength or valour of the enemy, nor to the cowardice of the citizens, nor, indeed, to his own timidity or helplessness; but that their danger lay in the very fact of their bravery, which, conscious as they were of their prowess and victories, had led them to oppose such a multitude of the enemy with too small a force of soldiers. "For," said he, "accustomed as I am to victory, and unacquainted with defeat, I should have thought myself beaten if I had been but a little more tardy in gaining a fresh victory over the enemy. For when, by Divine grace, the Norwegians and their King, who had overrun our territory from the north, were slain by us, and our armies and generals had been dismissed to their own homes, suddenly the Normans came upon us from the south. And I, meeting them hastily with a small force, not inferior in courage or spirit, but only in numbers, at length fell; but though conquered, I did not yield. No uncertain victory, then, shall we gain immediately over such as these, whom accident, and not bravery, has on this occasion shown to be our superiors. And to the attainment of this end, the enemy's insolence, and the manner of their unexpected attack, will prove the devotion of my people, and give consolation to our enraged army."

With these and similar arguments he importunes the Saxons, as well as the Danes whom he visited with an equal anxiety, to secure their help in driving out the invaders from his kingdom. But when he saw that their interests were directed into other channels, he was at first disturbed by, and gave himself up to, the agitations of a great anxiety. For he who was now King of the Englifh, as well as Duke of the Normans, in his forefight for his own fecurity had been thoughtful and prudent enough to anticipate Harold by haftening to ally himfelf, by means of an embaffy, in friendfhip with the King and nation of the Danes, as well as with the neighbouring countries, and to conciliate their favour.

*CHAP. VI.—How at length, coming to himself, he perceived that God was opposing him in his worldly path; wherefore, conforming himself to the Cross of Christ that he might the better triumph over the old enemy, he rejoices that he has suffered defeat at the hands of men.*

OW Harold, coming at length to himself, and returning, as it were, from his fantastic dream, is completely changed in his heart. He perceives, though late, that it was God who was opposing him in the way in which he was so fruitlessly walking, and that it was His angel's sword which had been borne against him and his obstinate efforts; and the eyes of his understanding being opened, he sees that he must choose another kind of warfare, and that other kinds of defences would be required. For the crucified King had looked upon the toils and long-sufferings of the dethroned King with a regard already favourable to him, and would not further suffer the special devotee of His banner to be engulphed in the depths, or

be overwhelmed in the maze of so great an affliction. He had beheld him fallen in sin and from his high dignity; and when He beholds, ruin ceases and the fallen arise. He had beheld, in short, that He might wash away his sin's fault with tears; yet He had not deprived him of the hope and desire of ruling, but had changed the nature of his desire.

He begins, then, to see his errors, and to lament the faults of his sins and wrong-doings in the sight of Him who sees all things: he begins to find that the path to a more blessed kingdom is far easier, and to have a foretaste of his opportunity. He is fixed in his mind to become an imitator of the Cross which he had loved, to bear his cross daily, to come after the crucified One, and to follow Him. Nor does it escape his notice that, in order to become fit for these things, he must first deny himself. As much as he can, then, he proposes to take Him for an example and a helper, who, though He was in the nature of God, stripped Himself of His divinity, and took the form of a servant. He now sees how the Lord of the world, when He was in the world, despised a worldly kingdom; and, when they sought to make Him a King, fled, and preferred the retirement of a solitary life to a throng of followers. He remembers that all power was given to Him in heaven and earth by the humiliation of a bitter passion and a cruel death. He foresees that this must eventually be undergone by all flesh. He remembers that all mankind must receive from Him an eternal kingdom or an eternal punishment. He knows that if he were to propose to make war against Him, and were to go against Him with ten thousand, that He would come to meet him with twenty thousand, whose unexpected coming and whose extraordinary preparations sometimes exterminate and destroy him whom He assails secretly and powerfully when He is least expected, and he who is unprepared for Him.

Putting on one side, then, his vain desire of a temporal kingdom, and casting off the fatal purpose of an earthly strife, he proposes to send an embassy to that King who is still far off, impelling him to inquire from Him what are the terms of a true peace. And fearing that His anger will be increased by his offences, and lest, perchance, his embassy alone may not be sufficient to propitiate Him, he resolves to seek out and entreat others, fitting and suited to the purpose, with all the prayers he can, to help him and interpose for him with the angry King, whose favour and glory alone he thought worthy of soliciting. Thus the outward appearance and inward disposition of Harold are both suddenly changed. The hand which he was wont to arm, he supports with a spear shortened into a staff. Instead of a shield, a wallet hangs from his neck. His head, which he was wont to equip with a helmet, and adorn with a diadem, is shaded with a head-dress. His feet and legs, in the place of sandals and greaves, are either altogether bare, or encased in stockings.

But let me relate the reſt in a few words: all the armour of the warrior, the whole adornment of this mighty man, is either left off altogether, or elſe worn for the humiliation and puniſhment of the penitent. Not only is the breaſtplate not thrown off from his ſhoulders, arms, loins, and ſide, but it is brought cloſer to his body; for the inner garments being taken off and thrown aſide, the roughneſs of the metal is next to the bare fleſh. Thus when awake, he walks, not indeed armed ſo much as impriſoned in armour. Thus when he ſleeps, a bed[1] does not receive him, but he is embedded in a cuiraſs. The change in the outer appearance which he aſſumed was wonderful. Pleaſant indeed was this great alteration in ſuch a man, both to the angels and all the ſaints; but far more pleaſing was the change wrought in the inner man by God the Judge, who created and formed in him light inſtead of darkneſs, and turned in a miraculous manner the man's whole nature.

In truth, I ſay, the change was not brought about by the hand of man, but by the right hand of the Moſt High, at whoſe word a cruel and ſavage nature ſoftens into mildneſs and gentleneſs, exaltation becomes humility; but who can tell of all the benefits of ſo bleſſed a change? That I may condenſe in a few words an endleſs matter: by this change, luſt of the fleſh and the world was transformed into a contempt and hatred of ſuch things, and yielded to a deſire and love for heavenly things.

[1] A play on the words "thorus" and "thorax."

Thus, I repeat, by the help of the Moſt High, the King is transformed into the ſoldier, and the ſoldier of Chriſt indeed, the kingdom of the world being now more deſpiſed than it was before deſired. The King is transformed into the ſoldier; the King becomes a ſoldier that ſo the ſoldier may become a king, and that he who is both king and ſoldier may be transformed into a king. The ſoldier begins to act a ſoldier's part on the ſide of Him for whom to fight is to be a king; to reign indeed in the preſent, and to reign with Him hereafter. For that reigning with Him is far better than this preſent reigning, for it is a far ſublimer and greater thing than reigning in the world and over a worldly kingdom. By becoming a ſoldier, indeed, he reigns, and by reigning he beomes a ſoldier, until the ſoldier of Chriſt changes all mutable things into things that endure, and death be ſwallowed up in victory, and battle be turned into a trophy. Then ſhall the King receive his kingdom, the ſoldier ſhall become a conqueror: the anxious man ſhall feel ſecure, and he that is mortal ſhall live for ever. Meanwhile the King and ſoldier thus changed, a new kingdom and a new warfare are given to Harold, the whole nature of his ſoul and body throughout every ſenſe and limb blooms afreſh and to new uſes in the world. In hunger and thirſt, in cold and nakedneſs, in prayers, in watchings, in inſults and wrongs; in a word, in every toil and hardſhip, the fleſh is weakened, the ſpirit ſtrengthened, the ſoul rejoiced. His panting breaſt trembles with sighs, which before swelled with slaughters and thundered forth threatenings. His eyes are bedewed with showers of tears, which were wont to flash forth lightnings on his rivals, at the bidding of an angry soul. His face, his brows, his neck displayed no elation, pride, nor cruelty; modesty regulates his gait; piety, his mind; purity guides his affections. Integrity gives form to his inward and outward movements; sanctity changes all his doings into her own ways. Harold appears now to govern himself more happily than is wont, to reign more eminently, to wage war with greater security and usefulness. He delights that he has been conquered by man, since by conquering the world and himself he has, though conquered, learnt how to achieve a more glorious victory over the devil.

CHAP. VII.—*How he entered on a long pilgrimage to obtain the prayers of holy men ; and how, before he became a King, he visited the resting-places of the holy Apostles.*

NSTRUCTED with an unction which now taught him concerning all things, he feels that he must carefully conceal that treasure of heavenly aspiration, lest, if published abroad thoughtlessly, it might be exposed to robbery. For firstlings of sheep or kine are not shorn nor put to the plough, and first-fruits were deemed unclean.

Therefore, instructed by such divine orders as these from the Holy Spirit, he leaves all his friends who had seemed to cleave to him up to that time: he deserts his kinsfolk : he retires secretly from all who had known him: he approaches peoples hitherto unknown to him : he seeks for supporters far and wide amongst those who are not unknown to him, but who were in days gone by indeed well known to and loved by him, and now more closely united in a feeling of devotion. This man, now a noble man indeed, departed then to a far-diſtant country to viſit ſacred places in order that he might pay honour to relics of the ſaints in their own homes and ſhrines; to obtain more fully and perfectly by their interceſſion the kingdom of God which he already held within his breaſt, intending after that to return to his own country.

Before this he had viſited the reſting-places of Chriſt's moſt exalted apoſtles, when he had not yet ſucceeded to the throne of the Engliſh, by an inſtinct of devotion indeed, but alſo with the object of bringing holy relics from their city to his own, rather than worſhipping them in theirs. For he had had a very fervent deſire to collect ſacred relics, eſpecially from the time he began to build and found the church of the Holy Croſs at Waltham, as we have narrated above; whence it happened that, having obtained numerous pledges of the ſaints, he appears alſo, by payment of vows and prayers and money, to have carried off from Rome on his return to his own country the bleſſed bones of the martyrs Chryſanthus and Daria. But the Romans, perceiving at length that they were being robbed of a great treaſure, and not thinking it right, follow the pious plunderer juſt as he is departing, or, indeed, had already departed three or four days' journey, and ſtop his progreſs. For a whole hoſt of the natives were not inclined to allow a few pilgrims to reſiſt them by force or break away in flight. What more ſhall be ſaid? Harold is ſtopped, bound, and overwhelmed with inſults, and he thought it hardeſt of all that he was compelled to give up thofe pearls of pricelefs value which he had lawfully obtained from their former poffeffors, as they indeed confeffed. Returning to his own country, then, for the violence of the Romans could not rob him of the prayers and favour of the above-mentioned witneffes of Chrift, and having managed to obtain, in fpite of all, fome very precious relics at Rome, he brought them home to be reverently preferved in the church which has fo often been mentioned.

And if anyone cares to know at greater length the watchfulnefs of his devotion and care in acquiring and preferving thefe relics of the faints, let him read carefully the treatife above-mentioned concerning the finding of the Crofs at Waltham. But we ourfelves, omitting what has been written by ancient writers, will give our pen a new duty, and follow, as we began to do, our new pilgrim, with Chrift for a guide. And if we are unable to accompany him to every place and on every fingle day as he wanders through many countries of Chriftendom and fpends fo beneficially his time; or if we do not know and cannot relate every fingle thing he did or fuffered on his long pilgrimage, let us at all events, following him as he is now already a long way off from our fhores, go and meet him as he returns to us with all fpeed. And let us give God higheft praife who was with him and guided him, and who at no time or place deferted him, and let us do honour to him in the Lord, who comes, indeed, in the name of the Lord.

*CHAP. VIII.—The admiration of the writer, with a brief exclamation on the goodness of God, by which it happens that the sins even of the elect work in them for good.*

EANWHILE, as Harold continues walking in the name of the Lord, his soul like a bride seeking her bridegroom, as he wanders through many places, and having found him, holds him, rejoicing with his spirit as it glories in God his Saviour, I seem to hear him singing with the psalmist, "Turn, my soul, to thy rest, for the Lord has shown favour to thee." But he, for joy of heart and admiration of the mighty acts of his beneficent Lord towards his servant, joyfully exclaims: O abounding piety and wondrous kindness of Thy Spirit! O virtue and wisdom! O co-eternal Son of an eternal Father! O sweet and blessed Jesus! O inestimable and unsearchable height of Thy counsels, truly no man can turn the thoughts of Thy heart. O how true were the feelings of her who said to Thee, "If Thou hast

decreed to fave us, we fhall for ever be delivered." How faithful, how worthy of acceptation is that faying, fo confidently uttered by Thy apoftle! "We know," he fays, "that all things work together for good to thofe that love Him." Bleffed be the holy name of Thy glory with the co-eternal Father and co-eval Spirit, who, when Thou wert angry, haft pity, and as the holy woman relates, forgiveft all the fins of mankind in their tribulation. And, indeed, all thefe things Thou haft fhown to be true, and countlefs, according to this meafure which are everywhere written in facred literature about Thee concerning thofe things which Thou doeft and fhoweft to thofe that love Thee, in this one man who loved and was loved by Thee. How plain the argument to us, how clear a fpectacle of gentlenefs and fortitude haft Thou built up in this one man! O Wifdom, who haft uttered words from the mouth of the Moft High, taking in hand with firmnefs all things from beginning to end, and difpofing them with gentlenefs! From thefe fprings of gentlenefs and firmnefs proceed thofe two rivers of grace and feverity or mercy and ftrictnefs, watered by which the furface of the earth of the faints, the tares being uprooted, brings forth its feed to the fruit of eternal life.

With what calmnefs and favour didft Thou take hold of this man, and, as fome think, on account of his wickednefs; yet didft thou not hurl him into eternity, but, taking hold of him and correcting him, broughteft him forth from his very iniquity to be more careful for himself, more devoted to Thee. What gentleness and what firmness didst Thou exercise with him, snatching him so powerfully from the hand of death, and not allowing his life to be taken away by javelin or sword, but restoring and re-creating in him the life of his soul, a life, as has been shown, deprived of its sin. Hence, too, his unrighteousness was found to abound to Thy glory, since out of the great and manifold sweetness of Thy kindness, where his wickedness abounded, Thy grace abounded more and more in him, in order that in proportion as he should love Thee more, he might receive a fuller pardon from Thee. That it might appear plain that not some things but all things work together for good to him who loves Thee, and even one's own great sin, which indeed is always evil, worketh to such a man to his eternal benefit.

CHAP. IX.—*How many things are said by many people about Harold's sin; and concerning the oak hard by Rouen, under which he made the oath, which remains, though stript of its bark, to this day.*

ONCERNING this man's sin, since many historians say much about it, we also ought to speak, and bring forward for impartial consideration what those, who have a desire to exaggerate or detract from it, think on the matter. For the majority accuse him of having committed a sin of no common kind; but of such heinousness, indeed, that they are of opinion the downfall of English liberty must be imputed to its enormity. For it is asserted that he took the name of the Lord God in vain, and feared not to pollute it with a false oath; and they also add that this act of sin was marked out by a wonderful miracle from heaven.

For the oak, which was once a tree of great height and beauty, as is proved by those who behold it to-day, under which Harold made the oath to the Duke of the Normans, as soon as he usurped the kingdom which he had sworn to preserve for him, and thus broke his oath, is stated, wonderful to relate, to have shed its bark, and to have lost its greenness and its foliage. A sight well worth seeing, for a tree which was a little time before remarkable for the number and thickness of its leaves, shrivelled up from the roots, as quickly as did the gourd of Jonah and the olive of that other prophet, and all its branches became white. The lasting nature of the withered tree, an indestructible oak, increases the miracle of the blight falling upon it, and this we have frequently, in common with many more, wondered at.

Who, indeed, would not be amazed that this oak, of such vast magnitude, not weakened by small branches but everywhere unbroken, from the lowest roots to the topmost leaves, thus stripped of every covering of bark, had not already yielded to old age and course of time; or wasted by decay, or beaten upon by the violence of the winds, and flooded by many rains, had not grown rotten or, at least, bent! But when we saw the tree one hundred and forty years after this event, when it was still to be seen thus marked, a man of Rouen declared that the crime of so enormous a perjury had been thus signalized by Heaven. The ill-fated tree still stands at a short distance from the city itself, overhanging a pleasant glade, which is not far from the bridge over the Seine stretching towards the hermits of Grandmont. The man of Rouen is said to have presumed, at the unusual omen, that London would first be subdued.

The whole of Neuftria, in like manner, learned to hope that the vaft riches of the Englifh might fubferve the waftefulnefs of her needy and greedy miftrefs. To this is added, by thofe who inveigh againft Harold, already truly a conqueror, the overthrow, as eafy as it was cruel, and as rapid as it was undeferved, whereby he unexpectedly loft his kingdom. Thus, without fufpecting it, he efcaped deftruction by only juft preferving his life.

CHAP. X.—*The excuse some make for Harold, whereby, exonerating him from perjury, they assert that it was with the sanction of God and consent of the holy Edward that he became King; and concerning the vision of the Abbot Elsin, in which the holy Edward declared that Harold should be conqueror over the Norwegians.*

N the other hand, some people, for the same reason (and frequently even before this many were of this opinion, estimating the act of the beloved man of God by the marks of divine favour which shone around him), endeavour to bring forward a reason for the non-fulfilment of the oath, and that Harold was quite right in assuming the kingly power. For judging from what happened after, if what he had sworn had been observed, it would have been beyond a doubt a disastrous thing to the nation, as it was against his own wish, and disadvantageous to the safety of his people. For he made the oath under restraint of fear, which fell upon this steadfast

man, who very rightly refufed to meet an immediate death, or a never-ending imprifonment. And befides, there appeared no other way out of the difficulty, confined as he was in a foreign country, and in fuch powerful hands; therefore, yielding to the dictates of human frailty, which never gives up life willingly, and to the advice of fome friends who were with him at the time, he took the oath thus prefented to him, to which both human laws and the divine canon are known to have condefcended through various neceffities of this life.

Concerning the right of extorting this oath, others will difpute as they pleafe. But it was lawful for him not to fulfil an oath thus forced from him, if, which none deny, the oath itfelf were illegal; and by its means, for he could not have done fo otherwife, he efcaped from the Normans who were keeping him prifoner. And when he at length was reftored to his own people, he told everyone openly what he had fuffered and what he had done. And when they hear his account they are all with one mind feized with rage, reject an agreement made under compulfion of an oath, and cry out vehemently that it muft not be obferved. Heaven forbid, fay they, that we fhould ferve the Normans! Heaven forbid that the liberty of our city and of our Englifh nobility fhould ever be fubfervient to the barbarian yoke of Norman pride! Why fhould more be faid? All cry with one voice: one opinion is in every mind. Putting afide, then, all danger from the oath, which was thought to be of no value,

Harold at length, by the unanimous advice of all, is raifed to the throne. But that this had not happened with the divine Will had been declared a little time after from heaven. For when the Norwegian King, failing with a numerous fleet, had made an entry into England, attacking the province of York with fire and fword, and had begun to lay wafte everything that came in his way, and when the newly-elected King was haftening to meet him with an army he had collected, he was fuddenly feized with moft violent pain in his leg.

Fettered as he thus had become, and in agony for the peril of his fubjects rather than at his own pain, paffing nearly the whole night without fleep in fighs and prayers, he begged for the familiar affiftance of the Holy Crofs. In the fame night there appeared to that fervant of the Lord, Elfin, the Abbot of Ramfey, King Edward, the holy and watchful defender of his people, the predeceffor of our forrowing and afflicted hero, telling the Abbot the misfortune of the King which had happened to his body and fpirit, fhowing him befides the King's thoughts as he lay upon his bed; fending him, and faying to him, "Rife, go, and tell your King from me the remedy for his prefent pain and the threatened war, that, at my interceffion, God has granted him the victory. Let the revelation of his heart's thoughts be a fign to him from heaven that the remedy is to be attended to, and let the argument of this unwonted revelation be a certain omen of his obtaining the victory." So the King, to fpeak briefly, is cured by divine favour, and is exhilarated by heavenly meſſages. Attacking the enemy with confidence he eaſily conquers them, for he overcame not by his own ſtrength, but by the might of Him who heals thoſe that are broken in heart, and binds up their wounds, deſtroying with the ſword the enemies of thoſe that love him. Therefore we gather by the perſuaſion of an argument which is not improbable, becauſe he obtained the kingdom by the connivance of his moſt holy predeceſſor and the ordaining of God, that, fortified as he was by the favour of the ſaint and adviſed by his divine meſſage, God Himſelf aſſenting thereto, he thus deſerved to gain a triumphant victory over his haughty foe.

CHAP. XI.—*A wonderful account concerning a Holy Crofs which is alleged to have bowed its head to Harold as he was haftening to battle; and certain other very aftounding miracles concerning this Crofs, proved to be undoubtedly true.*

NOT only was his legal affumption of the kingly power defended by thefe events and figns, but his favourable performance of the fame is proved. For, by a fign new and quite unheard-of in all ages, the clemency of the Saviour deigned to fignalize His own peculiar fervant in a more exalted manner for the fecond time, by which act of fo fignal a miracle, the favour and love of Heaven were difplayed to the devoted King, and his honour defended for ever againft the reproaches of defamers. The circumftance which happened was noifed about everywhere, as was its due, and is vifible to the eye to the prefent day. As he was returning from the flaughter of his enemies, this moft valiant King, haftening to meet fome new adverfaries who had attacked him, no preffure of hafte would allow

him to pass by his beloved church. He turns aside to it in his devotion, enters, prostrates himself, and the innermost feelings of his heart becoming softened, he worships the Holy Cross, multiplies vow upon vow of thanks for the victory he had just gained, and humbly doubles his prayers that he may obtain another trophy of victory, if it should please God's High Majesty. His prayers being at length finished, and the issue of the impending conflict entrusted in his earnest devotion to the faithful judgment of Him who orders all things, as he was on the point of returning with bent head and stooping body, and saying farewell to the Holy Cross, he bowed himself, as the custom is, and in response the countenance of the crucified image bowed itself.

This wonderful and auspicious action of the Saviour gladdened while it terrified some of those who stood by. For what could even be conceived more auspicious than that the immortal King of Eternity, though invisible, should be seen to answer the salute of a King of miserable mortals, and should deign and have the power to incline His head to him! How terrible this was to human weakness to see such strange things, that, contrary to all nature, a stone should bend; and, what is beyond nature, that God in His own image should be seen to bend to a human being! And what shall we say of this, that, where the art of man could not pierce even the thin palm of the divine image, the image itself was seen to bend its bodily neck? The workman toils and draws blood, and makes a hole in the hand of ſtone. A man, deſtined ſoon to be a King no longer, prays, and the neck of ſtone which, although it might by ſome means be pierced by man's hand, could by no means be bent, ſuddenly bends itſelf, yet is not broken ; bows itſelf, but from the completeneſs of the whole body or the joined head, not the ſlighteſt crack is made. And not only in the mere material was this great miracle ſo remarkable. For the image being of ſtone inſide, and the outſide ſilver, a double miracle was performed and diſplayed. It was the image, forſooth, of Him of whom it is written: "They have ſipped honey from the ſtone, and oil from the hardeſt rock." The ſubſtance indeed was of ſtone, yea, of very rock, hardeſt in quality, thick about the ſhoulders, neck, and arms of the image, and, ſo to ſpeak, corpulent.

This image was diſcovered by divine revelation, buried in the earth on the top of a certain hill ; nor was it known how or by whom it was faſhioned, or depoſited and concealed there. It was brought by divine command direct to the place we have ſo often mentioned, where theſe things are ſaid to have occurred, by oxen, who drew the cart on which it was laid about one hundred and twenty miles, and they would not allow it to turn aſide anywhere from the journey it had undertaken. There it was covered with ſilver plates, and was not joined or fixed to the lofty croſs. For it allowed ſo little of man's workmanſhip on it, that a man could not even make the holes for the nails to be driven in. Nor was this attempted, but the palm of the right hand, as foon as a little of the furface had been bored by an iron, was found to poffefs a foftnefs whence it emitted blood; but it loft not its hardnefs, whereby it repelled the hardeft auger. The right hand of the Lord gave this quality to the right hand of His image, which, as the Pfalmift fang, hath given ftrength, whence alfo it is a fitting quality of this material right hand, that being made illuftrious by fo many figns, and glorious by fo many prodigies, it may feem to declare, not fo much in words as in fact, "The right hand of the Lord hath exalted me; the right hand of the Lord hath given ftrength."

Now, we have related all this to the end that the manifold nature of the heavenly power might appear, which was fhown in this bending of the facred head of the holy image; for, as we have faid, in the filver as well as the ftony fubftance, this wonderful act of heavenly condefcenfion and power fhone forth to our eyes, which we can ftill behold to-day near the horn of the altar where the occurrence happened. For the ftone did not crack, nor did the filver plate experience a cleft, or contract a wrinkle, though it was ftretched to an unwonted degree from that part of the neck through fuch a bending; nor was it feen to be folded in the leaft proportion from the region of the neck and jaw. But there was an alteration, and not a fmall one, from its original pofition, for whereas the chin of the image, as we have formerly heard, ftood ftraight out, we fee it now hangs down and fettled upon the breaft, by reafon of the bending which we have defcribed.

*CHAP. XII.—Different interpretations of different men concerning the above-mentioned figns of the bowing Crofs and the withered oak; and how Harold, by judging himfelf, favourably anticipated the divine judgment and fears not man's.*

LTHOUGH this wonderful work of piety feemed at the time to have portended a happy and aufpicious omen, yet fome people afterwards faid that it prefaged an unlucky and difaftrous event. For when, a fhort time after, the King was beaten with his army, many thought that the bending of the image fignified the fubjugation of the Englifh and the lamentable downfall of the kingdom. But to thofe who look into the order of the occurrences and the fervices of the pious King towards the Crofs, both before and after the event, the former interpretation of fo divine an action feems more probable and more liberal. For God, who always gives in excefs of the merits and prayers of His fuppliant, is wont to liften to thofe who pray to Him as foon as they afk beyond what

they afk and underftand. Wherefore He turns a deaf ear oftentimes to what His petitioners wifh, but anfwers their prayers for their good and fafety; for it is only His enemy's wifhes that He grants to their own deftruction.

But it is not neceffary to make a long tale by narrating how He has anfwered the prayers of fome of the elect as well as finners. It is fufficient to bear in mind that the chief of reprobates fought to tempt that holy man Job, that this was accepted now and again, but was anfwered to the augmentation of his own condemnation. Let it fuffice to call to mind, on the other hand, that He, the chief of all the elect, when the fting of His fuffering was at hand, afked that the cup might pafs from Him, but obtained not the prayer which He had made according to His wifhes, but fubjected His will to the good pleafure of the Father, yea, and rendered it completely in fubjection. "Not My will," said He, "but Thine be done." For God in fuch a wifh as that, fpared not His own Son, giving Him up for us all, that He might on that account, when he had drunk of the brook in the way, lift up His head which He bowed upon the Crofs. The ftory of the confummation was declared to be the overthrow of the enemy of mankind. And on this declaration becoming known, He bowed His head in peaceful flumber, after the long vigils of an anxious conflict; and fweetly refted in peace after the agony of His bloody fweat. But thefe things unbelievers have interpreted contrari-wife. When He achieved the victory over His enemies, defeated fpite thought that it had conquered the victorious King. But He, knowing what He had done, bent His invincible head, which in victory He carried erect, in a fecure and peaceful fleep. It is now plain by this diftinguifhing fign the King had fhown, in bending His head to the fuppliant King, that He had granted him a better victory than the reft looked for or thought. For, left an erroneous opinion fhould prevail with the conquered againft the conqueror, and left He who was faid to be the King of the Jews fhould be thought to have loft His kingdom, there was added the governor's difapproval of the rafh opinion in letters, in the infcription placed over His head, which was already bent. For it was written there, "Jefus of Nazareth, King of the Jews." He remained, in truth, a king, for the wicked multitude envied Him His kingdom, and killed Him, fo that He bowed His Head. But He indeed bowed His head, affuming at the fame time the power of His kingdom; which confeffing[1] that He had received in its fulnefs, He exalted His bowed head above the heavens.

Let no one think that the royal name or royal dignity (to whom fuch a mark was fhown by the King of all Kings) was loft by the King, either becaufe He deigned to bow in his own image or becaufe it was not permitted the fame King vifibly to triumph over his threatening enemies by the fame means. But if anyone thinks that the

---

[1] Convefcens, *lit.* eating together with; here evidently a corrupt reading, perhaps for confeffus.

presage of such an unexpected virtue signified the extension of the kingdom, whose temporal administration was at first conferred on him, and afterwards taken from him, we do not deny that the downfall of English prosperity, and the overthrow of the liberty of the laity as well as the Church, which was experienced from that time, was portended to the inhabitants of our island. But the Holy Cross does not suffer the rights of its servant to be diminished because of its greater consideration for him.

But the eternal and unchanging God offers and promises to His worshippers for their labours and their religious worship not transitory and perishable things, but rather stable, good, and eternal things. Therefore the King granted, gave, and yielded to the King what he wished. And if he could in any other or better way have known how to give or grant it, it would have been the heavenly granting to an earthly one, a permanent for ever and ever to a transitory one. But He took away a shadowy kingdom from him for whom He preserved a true and everlasting one, that the former might not be even a slight hindrance to his passing to the latter. And lest the thoughts of men (whose foresight regarding impending danger is full of fear and doubt) should imagine that the good Lord purposed to such an extent to bring affliction instead of peace on his devoted servant, He resolved that the vastness of the miracle which He had performed should anticipate the enormity of a future offence, and that we might put a limit to such things as these, He deigned to bestow and confer the manifestation of His clemency on His servant. By these benefits, in fine, the exalted power, the infinite holiness, the unapproachable sublimity of the mercy and greatness of Almighty God the Father, Son, and Holy Ghost, the one and only King of Eternity, displayed on the King's diadem a pearl of great brilliancy, when he was under a cloud of persecution and in a slough of despondency.

And as for what some allege about the oak, let those attend to that who worship the beasts of the forest and trees, and who fear not nor blush to prefer the senseless wood and the brute beasts to men, partakers of their own nature, made after the image of God, and what is more than this, redeemed by His death. Let them take care lest perchance the tree itself foretold an omen for him who enforced the oath and his immediate posterity rather than for him who took the oath. Let them consider and decide whether it seemeth fitting to them by whose agency the bloom and vigour of the sanctity and liberty of the ancient Church of England wasted and vanished, that, when the first pulse of the kingdom began to beat, a green and leafy tree dried up, cast off in a moment its beauty, and displayed a perplexing nakedness.

But let it suffice that we have touched upon both sides of these matters which are related to have happened by some in favour of King Harold, and by others in opposition to him, leaving the settlement of the question to the final decision of the reader, or rather of the immortal God who knoweth all things. As far as we have been able, we have tried by means of what we have related, and which appeared to us not irrelevant to the fubject, to remove the ftumbling-ftones from the way, and to make the path plain, the actual facts, as we truft, guiding us.

It remains for us now to go and meet, with what fpeed we may, our King and patron, who is returning to us from his long journey, and to follow him to the beft of our power with the devoted fervice of our trufty pen, as he returns home firft to the home of the Angles and then of the Angels. But he himfelf, by accufing and judging himfelf, ftrove fo to anticipate the judgment of man and of God that it mattered very little to him to be judged by thofe who, according as they were difpofed towards him by hatred or goodwill, judge according to their human lights, generally wrongly, and feldom rightly.

CHAP. XIII.—*How, after many years spent abroad, Harold, returning to England for the purpose of exercising his patience and meekness, caused himself to be called* CHRISTIAN, *and lived ten years in a certain rock in solitude; with a short invective against the Antichrists of that time.*

FTER spending many years in the holy labour of a religious pilgrimage, Harold decided to practise a new method of life upon his body, worn out as it was with long toils and old age. He had learnt, indeed, the countless virtues and most holy lives of the saints whom he had visited, and he now resolved to stay his steps, to make an end of his wanderings, to bid farewell afresh to the activity of Martha, and to rest quiet, like Mary, in meditation on the sayings and doings of holy men which he had heard and seen, that he might the more lavishly enrich his spirit, so as to be able to sing with the Psalmist in deed and in truth, "That my soul may be filled with marrow and fatness, and my mouth praises Thee with joyful

lips." He had experienced and maintained in his own perfon, and in the fweet and gentle fanctity of the righteous, how gentle and pleafant is the holy of holies; and he thinks that it would be beft for him to reft in future, that he may fee more perfectly, and know in a more bleffed way, that the Lord Himfelf is God.

But left this bodily repofe (as is cuftomary to the thoughtlefs) fhould bring lazinefs or torpor upon his mind, he elected to reft and repofe in that land, by refiding in which he forefees that he will be able to poffefs and difplay a greater exercife and a more effective proof of his patience and goodnefs. He knew that the height of perfection, which he felt in his enlarged breaft in all its fulnefs, would ftand out moft clearly in that faying which the only begotten Son of the Moft High deigned to utter and teach the brothers of his adoption, "Pray," faid He, "for them which defpitefully ufe you and perfecute you; do good to them that hate you, that ye may be the children of your Father which is in heaven, for He maketh His fun to rife on the good and on the evil, and fendeth rain on the juft and on the unjuft." He afpired, therefore, in his heart's affection to the merit and reward of that true perfection to which he ought the rather to ftrive, and to remain in that land which contains as many of his perfecutors as there are dwellers therein; as many of his haters as there are men therein; almoft as many revilers as men who fpeak with him and of him. But he does not truft himfelf to fo ferious a ftruggle, nor commit himſelf to ſuch a danger without due conſideration; for he is well aware of the ſtrength of Him who dwelleth in him, and in whom he dwells; nor did he fear to ſay with the Apoſtle, "Since ye ſeek a proof of Chriſt ſpeaking in me." With full truſt, then, in the knowledge that he has ſuch a gueſt within him, he wiſhed to be called CHRISTIAN by name, that, being already joined in a union of the Spirit, he might alſo be united in the communion of name to Him who, he knew, was dwelling in him, ſpeaking in him, working in him, and ſuffering in him. For he ſaid with Paul, in his heart to himſelf, but to us alſo in work, "I can do all things through Him who ſtrengtheneth me."

It is not thus with the wicked man, nor with thoſe whom a treacherous enemy—an enemy who overthrows and is overthrown—arms only to deſtroy, ſtrengthens only to make weak. For ſuch an one teaches you to place your reliance in your own fleſh, that your heart may be alienated from God; that you may be like the tamariſk, blooming yet barren; and that you may dwell now in a land of ſaltneſs, which yields no fruit to its cultivators, and afterwards in an uninhabitable land, which gives no reſt to thoſe who dwell therein. In this land only eternal horror dwells. For who can dwell with the devouring flame, or who can abide with everlaſting fires? But theſe laſt prophetic words we uſe without abuſe, knowing the difference of thoſe fires: with which the one conſumes ſinners without deſtroying them; but the other, by confuming the fins, juftifies the finners, illuminating and kindling them. Yet why fhould we fpeak of thefe, of whom we are not concerned to fpeak or judge, who, indeed, rob and deftroy the church—aye, and churches—outwardly, but inwardly enter not into nor inhabit them—gathering the fruit and lopping the vineyard of the Lord of Hofts; but now they are cut down by the hufbandman, and, unlefs they grow wife in time, they are to be caft in a moment into eternal fire. Now becaufe thefe men are become Antichrifts, let us rather leave them to themfelves and their flame and return to our Chriftian. For even now, as the prophet witneffeth, the flame devours the enemy, and in obedience to the fentence of the true vine, the branch is afterwards caft into the fire and burnt.

But our Chriftian, new in name but old in profeffion, fecure in Chrift who dwelleth in him—already the victor of the world and of that Prince who is in the world—by a new warfare and a new art of fighting begins to conquer his conquerors. His King, with whom he had waged war already a long time in the hope of regaining his loft kingdom, had beftowed on him the flame of affection, with which, fanned by the breath of this Holy Spirit, the hammers of affliction had forged upon the anvil of fuffering a great panoply of victorious arms. With thefe he had learnt to fight without defeat for his loft kingdom—but a kingdom, indeed, in heaven, not on earth, knowing that, when he had obtained that, he could never lose it at the hands of any enemy. Led, then, at length to his former kingdom—possessed, indeed, with great danger, but lost to his great gain—ready to fight manfully with those weapons with which he was armed for a new and incomparably better kingdom, he enters the camp equipped with all his armour. For, retiring into a cavern hard by Dover, he first composed his mind, then, rising up out of himself, he beheld the land far above him, whose King sometimes his eyes could see in all His glory, in whom and with whom he presumed to have a certain hope of reigning.

Here, fulfilling all the commandments, he spent ten years of solitary life, like a soldier in his recruit service, and at length, becoming a veteran, he strove, by leading a godly life, to exceed even rather than fulfil the vital precepts of the Divine Law. For he knew that that was a life of virtue, this a life of holiness; that a life of beginning, this a life of perfection; that also he judged necessary, this glorious—here, in short, he looked for counsel, there for empire, for the safety of mankind, and at the same time for the glory of a jealous and favourable God.

Now this place, where he had thus determined to spend his life, was not far distant from the spot where he had formerly lost his earthly kingdom by nearly meeting his death, and by this act seized power from the Kingdom of Heaven. Here, therefore, the patience and gentleness of the man exercised and wasted his strength, where both his own and his people's paſt misfortunes, and the preſent pride of his enemies, was brought to his memory and ſight more frequently, foraſmuch as he was more urged in a more generous ſpirit to repay, not evil for evil, but the bounteous gifts of his holy interceſſion.

*CHAP. XIV.—How Harold afterwards spent a long time in various places on the borders of the Welsh, bore their repeated assaults in patience, hiding his face with a cloth, and changing his name for another lest he should by some means be recognised; how at length the cruelty of his persecutors was changed into veneration for him.*

IVING, then, among the Welsh, although he had been at one time an object of hatred to them, on account of what seemed at the time a just defence of his own race, he now desires, as Christian, to suffer with Paul what he had, as Harold, done with Saul. Bidding farewell, then, to Kent, he proceeds to Wales, and staying there in various places a long time, he lived with the Welsh and prayed for them, although they, without provocation, ceased not to assault him, who was now not fighting against them, but for them. But as he was going into a land, as we have stated before, where he was once known, he concealed both his features and his name, wearing

always in public the veil of a little piece of cloth before his face, left, if he were recognifed by any, the offer of their adoration to the merits of his virtues might lead him to become vain. If, then, his name were afked, he would fay that men called him Chriftian. He, indeed, difguifed both his face and his name, becaufe his name was known to all, and his face to many. For he was afraid that he might be betrayed by thefe indications, and he feared left he fhould be greeted with applaufe from his own friends, if perchance any furvived, or by ftrangers even, if he were recognifed, either at the contemplation of his former dignity and prefent humility, or under pretence of friendfhip or familiarity.

But it was not to be feared that, even if he were betrayed by his enemies, he would be treated in a hoftile manner, leading fuch a life and behaviour as he was doing, or put into clofer reftraint than he had put himfelf. Yet it was very probable, if his fecrets were known, that he might be troubled by what was worfe than tortures or imprifonment, namely, praife and applaufe. For who would not fhow all the reverence and honour he could to fuch a man, when he faw how lowly-minded and mild—how kind-hearted and gentle—how indifferent to worldly things—he was; and how, by his own free-will, he had become an object of contempt to lovers of the world, efpecially if it were no fecret that in former times he had held a confpicuous pofition in the world, and had been rich and powerful? And this is remarkable about his frugality and patience, that he did not fo much bear wrongs with patience, as repay them with kindneffes; and that he did not fo refrefh his faft-decaying body with food, as juft keep it alive. On this matter we have heard fully, from a certain holy fervant of Chrift, that if he were at any time eating a lean and fmall fifh, he would never eat but one half of it, leaving the other half untouched—not even turning it over, but would hand it juft as it was to his fervant, or to fome needy man, if one were prefent. By thefe ftrict refolutions this holy man, following the example of Him whofe Name he claimed to fhare, preferred to be defpifed and afflicted for a while with Chrift, and for Chrift, fince now he was called Chriftian from Chrift, rather than be enervated by the favours and pleafures of the world; for which reafon he had of his own free-will expofed himfelf to the favage company of the Welfh, putting before his mental vifion that Pafchal Lamb who freely offered Himfelf to wicked priefts to be facrificed for us.

For, defiring to walk as Chrift walked, this Chriftian haftened to follow wherever He went, through the purity of a worldly heart, and fuffering of an afflicted body, that Lamb, which perchance he could not follow in the unfoiled cleannefs of the flefh. For burning with a love of fuffering, as if he thought of too little account all the hardfhip and faftings he brought on his own body, himfelf his own torturer, he chofe to enter into companionfhip with a wild race, at whofe hands he knew he fhould be fubjected to many afflictions, if not indeed crucifixion itfelf. He fuffered, in truth, from thefe treacherous, favage, and defpicable men, only what he looked for and expected, for he was often violently beaten with very cruel ftripes at the hands of robbers, from whom alfo he fuffered every poffible injury. They pilfered his provifions, and robbed him of his clothes; and to induce him to bring forth money, of which he had none, they tortured him with exceffive and exquifite torments and ill-treatment.

Such, indeed, was the conduct of thefe men, or rather wild beafts, that that faying of St. Gregory concerning the Longobardi fuits their cafe exactly: "Whofe very compacts are punifhments, and whofe favours are fwords." But the man of God bore it all with a tranquil mind, a cheerful countenance, a gentle voice, and a generous hand. Nor did his pious habits ceafe, though he had to ftruggle with fuch impiety, until the evil of the latter was overcome and put to fhame by the goodnefs of the former, and glory and honour was heaped upon the piety which had won the victory. For he gave food and drink to his enemies, as the Apoftle tells us to do. He foftened the hearts of his defpoilers by kindneffes—he made his tormentors gentle by his wondrous, unheard-of meeknefs. He heaped, fo to fpeak, from the furnace of a great affection, coals of fire upon their heads, fo that the hardnefs of their hearts, foftened to the marrow, was at length melted, and they began to worfhip and honour him whom they had been accuftomed to mock and fcourge. The hand which once raged with ftripes, is now conſtant in kindneſſes. The tongue, once uſed to contumely, redoubles its praiſes. For the virtue of his not yet experienced goodneſs, after the manner of perfumes, the more it was handled, the ſtronger ſcent it had, and being widely diffuſed, the odour of his life became, by its diſperſion, life to many. For the ſweet fragrance of his holy reputation, gliding into their ſenſes, drove away and put to flight that devil's breath of raging miſt from the hearts of theſe brute beaſts, though human beings; and you might well think that ſuch an utterance as this came from their tuneful hearts, rather than their voices: "In the odour of Thy ointments we run, for our ſouls have loved Thee."

*CHAP. XV.—How Harold, the man of God, avoided the obsequious who persecuted him, whom he had approached, and long borne with; and how a place of rest was appointed for him by a voice that fell from heaven; and how he hinted in ambiguous words to those who asked him that he was Harold; and how the truth of the matter will be shown more fully in the account given by his successor.*

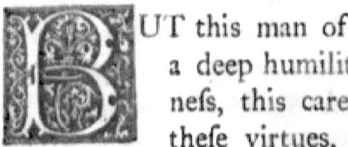UT this man of God, this practiser of a deep humility, this lover of quietness, this careful guardian of both these virtues, lest he should lose or destroy in the least either of these good qualities, decides that he must fly from those whom he had first sought out to persecute him, but who now were inclined to worship him. The virtue of his bodily strength, which would not yield to labours, but was become broken with years, began to give way in him. Once you would have thought that his knees were growing strong rather than weak by his fastings; that his legs were gaining activity;

that he scarcely felt fatigue. But now the decrepit old man was to experience that "Old age brings everything." He makes a prayer to the Lord that he may be shown a place, in his declining years, desiring a pleasant vision to his fainting heart, and begs that God with His wonted kindness will grant him such a resting-place, where he may pass the remainder of his life in the quiet of a much-desired repose, and there end his days by a happy death. And feeling that the Lord in His beneficent spirit had listened to the pious desire of His poor suppliant, he caused himself to be mounted on a poor beast, and, content with his usual attendant, starts on the journey which the Lord would deign to appoint for him; and was thus borne by feet that were another's because his own had no strength left in them. Departing, then, ignorant by design, and wisely uninformed of his journey's end, and led by angelic guidance, he reached at length the city of Chester, where, as the day was declining towards evening, arriving in the midst of the city, when he heard his attendants inquiring where they were to stay, a voice suddenly falls upon them. "Go," it said, "good man, to the church of St. John; there you shall find a resting-place prepared for you." The attendant, astonished at what he heard, gazes all round with curious eye, seeking for the owner of the voice, but none was visible. It was clear, forsooth, that it was the Lord's holy angel who, accompanying them on their journey, and ordering everything for their benefit, had told the man of God that a place was prepared for him. And he, as was his cuftom, with the veil that hung before his eyes covering nearly the whole of his face, had difguifed his countenance, left he might frighten thofe who met him by the remarkable appearance of his wounds; or left, if he were recognifed, a feeling of vanity might fteal over his fenfes at the reverence he would be fubjected to. The byftanders foon point out with their finger the church which was fignified to them by the divine oracle; he approaches, and is heartily welcomed as a heavenly-appointed gueft.

For the fact was that a venerable hermit of that place had recently departed this life, thus leaving his little dwelling vacant for a holy fucceffor thus divinely provided. The daughter of Sion, by which I mean the church we have mentioned above, full of joy and gladnefs (though no one knew for certain who he was), received her King, though feated in this ignoble fafhion, and yet a faint, and coming in all things as a Saviour to them. And as he abode there, when he was frequently afked by thofe who came to vifit him, and who reported what edification they gained from him, whether he was prefent at the war when King Harold was faid to have been killed, he replied, "I was certainly there." But to fome who fufpected that perhaps he might be Harold himfelf, and who queftioned him more clofely than was right, he would fometimes thus fpeak of himfelf, "When the battle of Haftings was fought, there was no one more dear to Harold than myfelf." With fuch ambiguous words, fo to fpeak, he did not so much confirm the truth of the facts, as refuse to strengthen them in their doubtful conjectures. But how the evidence of the matter became at length plainly known to all will be shown below in the words, not of ourselves, but of a venerable man who succeeded Harold in his habitation at the same hermitage.

*CHAP. XVI.—The reader is advised not to despise the reading which he feels differs from the opinions of some; and concerning the three occasions of those who think differently about this present subject; and concerning the threefold mistake of William of Malmesbury on the fate of Harold.*

MEANWHILE, I think I ought in all humility to suggest to the reader that he should not think he ought to despise our history from its evident insignificance, because, perchance, he remembers that many persons have spoken and written on this same subject in one place or another; for it is plain that not only ordinary historians, but also most renowned orators, have thought and written not only differently, but quite the opposite to each other concerning the words of Harold. For it is quite clear, both by common-sense as well as authority, that what differs from truth cannot be true. This also St. Jerome, at the dictation of truth itself, has said. But in the reasonableness of these opinions which we are here ventilating, a threefold cause of difference of opinion or, what no one ought to deny, of falsehood, can be assigned by those who well consider the matter. In the first place, indeed, it is plain that, in many cases, the truth of matters has for a long time escaped everyone. Hence dislike of, or favour to, a particular person seems to have given an excellent opportunity to kindly-disposed persons of relating good things, and likewise to evil-disposed persons of inventing evil things, when the facts themselves were uncertain.

Actuated by some such consideration as this, that most eloquent William of Malmesbury discriminates in his chronicles, and promises to take a half-way position between Harold's detractors and his supporters. I should have thought he would, without doubt, have insisted on the truth for its very virtue's sake, and would not willingly have defrauded the merits of the affair of their just praises or their due criticism. But because he wrote of things he had heard of but had not seen, by the law of histories the truth of the writer is assured where the truth of the facts themselves is wrecked; otherwise, not even had the most blessed writers of the Gospels escaped the risk of mistakes—thus Joseph is called the father of the Saviour; thus certain of His disciples are more particularly called His brothers than the rest, not that their real father, but their putative father had them as sons, not indeed natural, but adopted sons. Therefore, following general opinion, and unaccuftomed to the truth, this man is known to have introduced into his hiftory what it is plain was the reverfe of the truth, however much the truth of things is relied on to ftrengthen one's ftory.

But in the other things, which he commented upon at one time with a pen of gold, at another with a pen fteeped with pitch, concerning the merits or manners of Harold, as his mind informed him or report fuggefted, perhaps he wandered from the path of truth fomewhat pardonably; but he fell more feverely when he attacked the very Anointed of the Lord. For he turned upon himfelf in his impetuofity three fpears, by which it chanced that, not his perfon indeed, but his truth was attacked. He faid that Harold met his death by an arrow-wound upon his head; he faid that the foldier who attacked the dead King's thigh had been driven from the army after cenfure from the victorious Duke; he related that money was offered by his mother to the victorious William for a royal funeral, but that he was taken away, without payment of money, and buried at Waltham. Thus, concerning the thigh, the head, and the man's whole body, the tongue of the fpeaker, who writes many things in fecret, runs riot with more licence than the armed hand of the foldier who fights openly. But the Lord has delivered the poor and needy man—whom He has proved to be more mighty in moft things than many orators and kings—from the arrow of the mouth of the one and from the fpear in the hand of the other.

I do not fpeak of all thefe things; but the Lord will give to him who walks in fimplicity the power to underftand what I write, to think what I think. But a contemporary of the prefent writer has written in temperate language an account of thefe things (namely, Ethelred, a venerable abbot) in the life of his holy predeceffor, King Edward. He fays, indeed, that Harold either fell in battle or efcaped, not without wounds, referved for repentance.

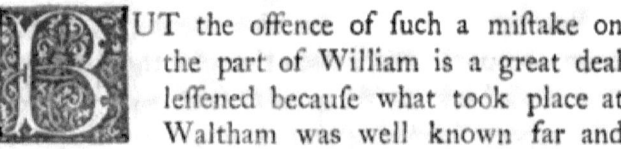

CHAP. XVII.—*What happened to the people of Waltham in their holy anxiety concerning the burial of their patron; and how they were misled by a woman's mistake.*

BUT the offence of such a mistake on the part of William is a great deal lessened because what took place at Waltham was well known far and wide. For, in truth, this horrible report had reached the ears of the private domestic canons of the King at Waltham, seeing that nearly everyone was saying that the King had fallen at the battle of Hastings. The clerks, so often mentioned above, not unmindful of the devotion due to their most generous patron, sent a certain woman of a shrewd intelligence, Edith by name, to the district where the battle had been fought, that she might carry away the limbs of their dead lord, to be buried reverently in their church. She seemed [a more suitable person] to make the attempt, insomuch as the weaker and less favoured sex would be considered less an object of suspicion to the cruel officers in authority, and more an object of compaffion. But this woman feemed more fitted than all others to carry out this affair, becaufe fhe could more eafily difcover amongft the thoufands of corpfes him fhe fought, and would handle his remains more tenderly, becaufe fhe loved him exceedingly, and knew him well, inafmuch as it was clear that fhe had been frequently prefent in the fecret places of his chamber. But when fhe reached the ill-omened fpot, fhe heard from many Normans, who were everywhere boafting, that the King of the Angles was ignominioufly beaten, with his crofs broken in halves, and that he was lying on the battle-field, killed amongft the flain.

But let the reader fee what turned out to be a truer account. For others thought that they who had carried off the King half dead, had fet about this report, forefeeing that it would be dangerous to them and to him, and would prove their certain deftruction, if the enemy fhould hear that he was alive. We muft not therefore wonder at the miftake of the woman who, unable to difcern the features of the body—hacked about as it was, covered with blood, already becoming black and decompofed, fince fhe could not find one which fhe could be certain was the King's—feized hold of, and carried off with her, another man's mangled corpfe, to fatisfy the public eftimation. And this was the body which was received in all reverence by the Canons of Waltham, without queftioning the truth of the matter, and was handed over for burial in the Church of the Holy Crofs.

*CHAP. XVIII.—How a brother of Harold, Gurth by name, replied to Walter the Abbot, or others, when asked concerning the ashes or the burial of his brother.*

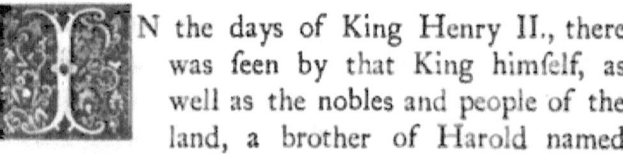N the days of King Henry II., there was seen by that King himself, as well as the nobles and people of the land, a brother of Harold named Gurth, whom the above-mentioned historian in his book relates at the time of the arrival of the Normans to have been in years little more than a boy, but in wisdom and uprightness of mind, almost a man. But he was, at the period we speak of, of a great age, and, as we heard from many who saw him at that time, beautiful to look upon, noble in mien, and very tall in figure. The Abbot of the regular canons at Waltham, the Lord Walter, of pious memory, was the first to see him; and was very eager to ask him, as well as his brothers, who were about the King's Court at Woodstock, whether in real truth the ashes of his brother were preserved in their

monaſtery, as was generally believed. He replied in Engliſh, "You may have ſome countryman, but you have not Harold." Yet he came to the place himſelf to worſhip the Holy Croſs, and when his brother's coffin was ſhown to him, looking aſkance at it, ſaid: "Man knoweth not" (for ſo he ſware). "Harold lies not here." May that Lord Michael, Canon of the approved religion, Chamberlain of the Church at Waltham, live long and flouriſh in Chriſt, who firmly aſſerts that he heard theſe words from the man's own mouth, while many ſtood by, ſome of whom ſtill ſurvive. Thus having diſcuſſed theſe things briefly and, as we truſt, not unprofitably, for the information of our readers, left the uncertain differences of writers ſhould diſturb them, we will now, as we promiſed, ſet down the words of the man we ſpoke of above, by which it is clearly taught how the goodneſs of Chriſt made plain by many ſigns the fame of His ſervant.

CHAP. XIX.—*How the successor of the man of God, writing a true account of the deeds of the most blessed Harold, has on two occasions assigned inappropriate reasons for his actions; with a discussion on the first reason, and a full disproval of the same by the production of the evidence of various opinions.*

E must consider that view also in the words of the most faithful relator, that, just as he lucidly explained things that were done, so he took care to express the reason of the things done not sufficiently fitly and prudently, as most people think; and this may be said without offence to such a great man. Hence, therefore, that third thing can be taken into consideration, which, as we said, gave rise to a ground of difference among the writers: I mean, the quality of mind or intelligence of those who relate all these things in order, who, according to the bent of their mind, measuring the affection of the most holy man, and the purpose of his actions, have taken on them-

selves to intimate the reasons of those actions. The evident credulity of these writers by careless expressions has darkened with an interpretation far from true deeds worthy of the highest praise. And this seems to have happened not once, but twice, to this good man in the course of his narrative, in their opinion who, fully relying on self-evident reasons and other persons' opinions—I mean the opinions of those who had clung more closely to the servant of the Lord—have impressed in some way or other more deeply on their hearts an inward likeness of his mind. But what those things may be, by which the course of that truth is not sufficiently established (as is thought) it is worth while to discuss briefly, to the end that we may remove from the midst of it all darkness of doubt, bringing to bear the force of our discretion, as far as we can, on our more simple-minded hearers.

Thus the aforesaid man says of the saint who was then on his journeyings, as follows: "Afterwards, because to live on one's own native soil is always pleasant, he made all haste to England, where he had formerly been King, that he might spend there the remainder of his days." But since it is a trite saying of the wise that that man is yet weak who holds his fatherland dear, but still strong when he makes any land his fatherland, and even perfect when every land is a land of exile to him; who does not see that it is absurd that a man withered with old age, as he himself says, and broken down by the length of his journey, religious though it was, fhould be declared to have been attracted by the fweetnefs of his native foil to feek a fatherland again in it? And does not the Lord fay to Abraham, "Get thee out of thy country;" and again in the Pfalm, "Forget thine own people and thy father's houfe"? And if the fweetnefs or recollection of his land, his people, and his father's houfe could not hold him of lefs age or inferior ftrength of mind, or holinefs of purpofe, would it lead or would it attract him to all thefe things whereby the more he advanced the more perfect he became? but would not that faying of the evangelift thunder in the fpiritual ears of the man who was pondering in his heart over the fweetnefs he had loft, "No man putting his hand to the plough, and looking back, is fit for the kingdom of God"? And again, the well-meaning writer does not confider what fort of a thing that native foil was to him—how it was ftill unchanged, how it was hoftile to him and his party, and how it could even feem to him to be irkfome when he looked back upon the whole of his life, even if he was ftill led along by an affection tenderer than ever.

CHAP. XX.—*The weakness of the second reason assigned, and the writer's warning to the reader; and on the difficulty of patching up materials torn indiscriminately by ancient writers.*

ND indeed he has no stronger ground to stand on, when he alleges the reason why he left Shropshire to go to Chester. He relates that he abandoned the place in which (as the writer maintains), though so cruelly and frequently afflicted in losses and stripes by the Welsh, he seemed to have settled, at peace with himself and giving thanks to God, for the space of seven years, in order that the outward tribulation might not destroy the repose of the inward man from its attitude of self-control. But this opinion is detected to be invalid, no less than the other, when considered, and when the tradition is accepted of those who assert that he dwelt in the country of the Welsh for this very reason, which describes how he suffered at the hands of those whom he had in past years afflicted with such utter devastation,

though with an apparently juft caufe, whatever the merciful difpenfation of God, who orders all things in kindnefs, had permitted him to fuffer. For if, under pretext of withdrawing him from fuch violence, he had refolved to change his abode, he would have done it fooner, and not have waited to be afflicted fo often with loffes and ftripes. For he was well acquainted with their fhores, in the midft of which, in a three-years' expedition, he knew them to their exceffive coft, as is related, thoroughly and entirely, as one fays. For this was the land which he had fubdued by his wonderful bravery, when yet an Earl, and nearly deftroyed it, which not one of the Kings who fucceeded him up to this prefent day had power to do.

For it is maintained that he poffeffed fuch ftrength, and withal fuch wonderful boldnefs that, as we read, not one of the armed Norman army approached to attack him, but both horfe and rider were overthrown by him at the firft blow, mortally wounded. This remarkable valour he had now put off, trufting now in the Lord, and flying with wings he had affumed, and nowhere failing in his flight. But the only thing he feared was that the power of his wings might be weakened by the lubricity of a worldly profperity, becoming feeble and not fo much like the birds whom God feeds as thofe men whom the wind feeds, if in his cafe the feven locks of Samfon fhould be fhorn by the razor of adulation. It was this alone he fled from, becaufe it was the only thing he feared; it was not, indeed, the weapons of the Welsh, but the oil of the sinner. He knew that the Welsh held the unknown in suspicion, but those who were approved in religion in veneration, and that therefore they despised the companionship of the one, and admired that of the other. But the man of God, now just and brave, now prudent and temperate, sought out those who despised him, that he might suffer justly what he feared he had deserved; and wisely deserted those who admired him, lest he should be deprived of the benefit of his temperate moderation. He remembered that the fire near the prophet suddenly burnt the beautiful, fertile, and fruit-bearing olive-tree, at the appearance of a loud voice; wherefore he wished to walk with the great and not amongst those who looked on him with admiration. Therefore he evades liars and sinners whom he had for a long time borne upon his back, when he saw they were hastening to strike on the head.

But now my story pleads for an ending. My book must be closed, that the pen of those who know these things more fully may narrate what it is necessary to be known concerning Harold. But let this little book in its last sentences implore the benevolent reader to deign to make allowance for the excesses of the author by holy prayers, and assisted by the intercession of the pious King Harold, let him take him in his company to the harbour of eternal safety; may he grant pardon for the garrulousness of the writer of this present work when he sees how very difficult it was to patch up and make new again the materials at his command, torn and misplaced as they are by the studies of former authors, and to guide into the wished-for haven the boat, old and shattered, amid the ill-famed rocks of histories, while the tongues and writings of calumniators are, as it were, winds fighting against it. But all glory and honour be to God our helper, who alone, the Trinity and Unity, is King, blessed, worthy of praise, glorious and highly exalted for ever.

## The Narrative of the Hermit

*who succeeded the holy Harold on the death of that most pious King, and the miracles which were performed by his means after he departed to the Lord, preceded by a short account of his doings and sufferings from the time he lost his earthly kingdom.*

T is written that tribulation worketh patience, patience experience, experience hope. For the experience of patience and confirmation of a pious hope, God sometimes permits His people to have tribulation in this life that He may free them from an eternal tribulation, wherefore He also allowed the venerable Harold, once King of the Angles, to have tribulation, and to be overcome by his enemies, and expelled from his kingdom, left he might grow proud because he had gained a victory; and left, having been raised to kingly power, he might put on one side the love of God because of his prosperity, but having been placed in poverty that he might live a more holy and blessed life, while he had his mind altogether free from earthly occupations.

Therefore, after the lofs of his kingdom, and the cure of the wounds he had received at the hands of the Normans, he takes a [journey] in the guife of a pilgrim to holy places through many lands, working for God on his holy pilgrimage. But after a time, being ftiff with old age and fhattered by his long journey, he became defirous to inflict on his weary body another form of religious practice. And becaufe to live on one's native foil is always pleafant, he made all hafte to England, where he had formerly been King, that he might fpend there the remainder of his days, poor, defpifed, and meanly clad, where once he had flourifhed as a king, wealthy, exalted, and clad in coftly garments, and in order that his merit might increafe in the fight of God (in proportion as he might poffefs a more benevolent fpirit) becaufe he would be able every day to look upon his adverfaries and be happy in the kingdom he had loft, and alfo to obey the Lord's command in praying faithfully to God for them.

On arriving at the fhores of his native country, he chofe the folitary life of a hermit, and living there in many places unknown to all till he made his laft farewell to earthly things, he miniftered to God by faith. Nor did he change his place of abode by any caprice, but he fought where he might ferve God with moft tranquillity. Now this fame noble man had formerly an attendant named Mofes, who, when I, the prefent writer, was confined in the fame place at Chefter, where the Lord Harold, the hermit and friend of God died, attended me alfo for two years. And I will tell you briefly and faithfully, though I muſt omit much, the events which follow according to the account of Moſes and other faithful men. At length the man of God came to Shropſhire, to a place called (Cefwrthin) Chef-wardine, and there for ſeven years leading the life of a hermit, with this Moſes for his attendant, he was very much diſturbed by Welſh robbers, and was frequently and violently afflicted at their hands by their robberies and aſſaults. All this he bore with patience, in all things giving thanks to God with humility. But after a time, left outward tribulation ſhould caſt him down from his poſition of control over his inward man, he left that place, and followed by the above-mentioned attendant, ſet out for Cheſter, and there, in the Chapel of St. James, which is ſituated on the River Dee, outſide the walls of the city in the cemetery of St. John Baptiſt, he ſpent a hermit's life with great ſtrictneſs for ſeven years, until his death. He wore for a long time a corſelet next his ſkin, till it was all rotten, and quite worn away. But the cuttings and looſe pieces he bade his ſervant throw ſecretly into the river, that it might appear to no man that he had worn it. In his body, indeed, he was moſt chaſte and continent: in heart, lowly and prudent. Of what ſtation of life he was he always kept a ſecret, that he might not by chance be held in too great veneration by men, whereby his mind being elated he might ſlip from the path of uprightneſs, and the merit of his humility might be diminiſhed in the ſight of God. He rarely quitted the chapel, but was conftant in continual prayer, doing what God has faid: that men ought always to pray and not to faint. In front of his eyes he hung at all times a cloth, which covered nearly the whole of his face, fo that when he wifhed to walk at all far he required the hand of a guide. Why he did this, his attendant did not know; but perhaps he did it to hide the appearance of the wounds upon his gafhed face, or left, if a free outlet for his eyes exifted, an opening for fecular vanities might be made for his foul, or elfe it was that he might not be recognifed and venerated by any who had feen him in former times.

ON THE LAST MOMENTS OF HAROLD.

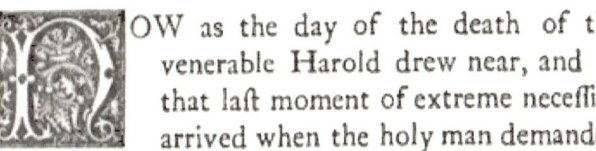OW as the day of the death of the venerable Harold drew near, and as that laſt moment of extreme neceſſity arrived when the holy man demanded the conſolation of the Holy Sacrament, a prieſt, whom I knew well, named Andrew, came and viſited the ſick man and adminiſtered to him all that the Chriſtian rite requires. But as he was liſtening to his laſt confeſſion, he aſked him of what ſtation of life he was? To whom he replied: "If you will promiſe me, on the Word of the Lord, that, as long as I live, you will not divulge what I tell you, I will ſatisfy the motive of your queſtion." The prieſt anſwered: "On peril of my ſoul, I declare to you that anything you ſhall tell me ſhall be preſerved a ſecret from everyone till you have drawn your laſt breath." Then he replied: "It is true that I was formerly the King of England, Harold by name, but now am I a poor man, lying in aſhes; and, that I might conceal my name, I cauſed myſelf to be called

Chriſtian." Not long after this he gave up the ghoſt, and now, conqueror over all his enemies, he has departed to the Lord. But the prieſt at once told them all that the man of God had confeſſed to him, in his laſt words, that he was indeed King Harold.

# INDEX.

Aillard, physician and abbot, 17, 18, 23
Alemanni, the, 18
Anchorite, at Chester, 78
Andrew, a priest, 98
Antichrists, 69

Benjamin, 29
Benoni, 29
Beseleel, 6
Brompton, the historian, 81
Butler, Alban, 44

Ceswrthin, or Cheswardine, co. Salop, 96
Chanaan, 28
Chester, city, 30, 77, 81, 95, 97
—— chapel of St. James, 97
—— cemetery of St. John Baptist, 97
—— chapel of St. John, 77
—— church of St. John, 98
Chophmos, 28
Chrysanthus, the martyr, 44, 45
Cnut, King, 13

Daci, the, or Danes, 13-15, 36, 37
Daria, the martyr, 44, 45
De, River, 97
Domesday Book, 34
Dover, 69

Edward the Confessor, 13, 15, 17
Ellis, Sir Henry, 35
Elsinus, the abbot, 55
Esdras, 3
Eyton, Rev. R. W., quoted, 96

Francalanus, 34

Germany, 35
Giraldus Cambrensis, 81
Godiva, Countess, 96
Godwin, Earl, 13-15
Grandmont, Priory of, 51
Gregory, St., 74

Hardy, Sir Thos. D., ix.-xi., 81
Harold, description of the MS. *Vita*, i.; history of the MS., ix.; notice of historical points and translation, xii.; pedigree of, 13
Hastings, xi., 78
Henry I., King, 26
Henry II., King, 51
Hiram, 6

Jacob, 29
Jeronymus, 79
Jerusalem, 3
Jonah, 51
Joseph, 28
Joseph, St., 80

Knighton, the historian, 81

Longobardi, the, 74

Martha, 66
Mary, Virgin, 66
Moses, 3
Moses, or Moyses, a servant, 95-97

Nehemiah, quoted, 3
Neustria, 24, 52
Normandy, 24, 29, 34, 54
Norway, 29, 36, 50, 54

Ooliab, 6
Oxfordshire, 31

Paralysis, 17
Paul, St., 70
Pedigree of Harold and William the Conqueror, 13
Prom Abbey, 45

Rachel, 29
Relics, 44
Rothomagus, 51

Saboth, 68
Samaritans, the, 34
Saracen, a, woman, 35
Saul, 14, 71
Saxony, 35, 36
Sebricht, anchorite, 30
Shropshire, 96
Stanton, in Oxfordshire, 31
Stephen VI., Pope, 44
Syon, 78

Uriah, 15

Wales, 17, 71, 73
Waltham, 19, 20, 24-26, 81
William the Conqueror, 13, 24-26
William of Malmesbury, 80, 81
W. Pictaviensis, the historian, 81
Winchester, city, 35

# ELLIOT STOCK'S PUBLICATIONS.

Now ready, in two vols., paper boards, price 10s. 6d., post free.
A *FACSIMILE* OF THE FIRST EDITION OF

## Rasselas, Prince of Abyssinia.

By Dr. SAMUEL JOHNSON. With an Introduction by Dr. JAMES MACAULAY, and a COMPLETE BIBLIOGRAPHY of the Work to the present date.

\*\*\* *Fifty large paper copies have been printed, price 21s. each.*

"The best tribute to the memory of Johnson which the centenary of his death has called forth."—*Athenæum.*

---

Tastefully printed on fine paper, with Illustrations in the highest style of Wood Engraving, price 9s., post free.

## Gray's Elegy.

Written in a Country Churchyard. With a *Facsimile* of the Fair Copy of the Original in the Author's Handwriting.

---

In large 4to., ancient MS. style, price 6s. 6d., post free.

## Shapira's Last: He, She, It.

An Episode in early Egyptian History. This wonderfully clever skit, which appeared in Germany a few months since, has been translated into English rhyme, with all the irresistibly comic illustrations given in the original.

"With its rough canvas cover, corroded seal, and leather thongs for clasps; the torn and broken edges of the imitation papyrus, stained and streaked as though by the hand of Time and the saturation of the waters of the Nile; marvellously quaint drawings, and generally dilapidated appearance, *He, She, It* offers a strange and diverting novelty to lovers of books at a reasonable cost."—*Daily News.*

---

In two vols., handsomely bound in cloth, price 18s.; in Roxburgh morocco, 21s.; large paper (50 copies only) 40s.

## Cornish Worthies:

Sketches of some Eminent Cornish Men and Families. By WALTER H. TREGELLAS.

"An excellent book, happily thought of, and happily brought to a successful issue."—*Morning Post.*

"The writer has aimed at interesting the general reader as well as giving the antiquary and the genealogist materials from which to glean valuable information."—*Western Antiquary.*

"Thanks partly to the superior sources of information within the author's reach, the work is the most complete extant; and the various essays or biographies constitute excellent reading."—*Cornubian.*

---

In crown 8vo., Contemporary binding, price 10s. 6d., post free.
THE LIFE AND STRANGE SURPRISING ADVENTURES OF

## Robinson Crusoe,

Of York, Mariner. Being a *Facsimile* Reproduction of the First Edition, published in 1719, with the curious Frontispiece, and a Preface by AUSTIN DOBSON.

---

ELLIOT STOCK, 62, PATERNOSTER ROW, LONDON, E.C.

# ELLIOT STOCK'S PUBLICATIONS.

In crown 8vo., 6s. ; old style calf, 10s. 6d. ; antique morocco, £1 1s.  Large paper copies, Roxburgh binding, £1 1s. ; antique Turkey morocco, £2 10s.

## Walton's Compleat Angler ;

Or, The Contemplative Man's Recreation. A Reprint of the First Edition, published in 1653.

---

In crown 8vo., old style binding, price 5s., post free.

## George Herbert's Temple.

Sacred Poems and Private Ejaculations. By GEORGE HERBERT, late Oratour of the Universitie of Cambridge.

This *Facsimile* is made from one of about twenty copies which were struck off for presentation to Herbert's friends, in 1633, before the issue to the public of the first published edition. Reproduced from Mr. Huth's copy.

---

In small 4to., antique binding, price 10s. 6d., post free.  Large paper copies, 21s.

## Milton's Paradise Lost.

A *Facsimile* Reproduction of the First Edition of 1667. With an Introduction by DAVID MASSON, M.A., LL.D., Author of the "Life of Milton," etc.

---

In crown 8vo., boards, or old style binding, price 3s. 6d., post free.

## Bunyan's Pilgrim's Progress.

Being a *Facsimile* Reproduction of the First Edition, published in 1678.

---

In crown 8vo., old style binding, price 5s., post free.

## Some Passages of the Life and Death of the Right Hon. John, Earl of Rochester.

Who died on the 26th July, 1680.

Written by his own direction on his deathbed. By GILBERT BURNET, D.D. Reprinted in *Facsimile* from the Edition of 1680. With an Introductory Preface by Lord RONALD GOWER, and Portrait.

---

Handsomely bound in vellum, small 4to., price 17s. 6d.

## A Noble Boke of Cookery.

A Collection of Quaint Recipes and Menus, throwing much interesting light on the Culinary Arrangements of our Forefathers. A Verbatim Reprint from a rare MS. of the fourteenth century, in the Holkham Collection. Printed in old style, and tastefully bound.

---

ELLIOT STOCK, 62, PATERNOSTER ROW, LONDON, E.C.

www.ingramcontent.com/pod-product-compliance
Lightning Source LLC
Chambersburg PA
CBHW021304240426
43669CB00042B/1315